Why
Doesn't
God Do
Something?

Why Doesn't God Do Something?

by Phoebe Cranor

DIMENSION BOOKS
BETHANY FELLOWSHIP, INC.
Minneapolis, Minn. 55438

Why Doesn't God Do Something
by Phoebe Cranor

Library of Congress Catalog Card Number 780118

ISBN 0-87123-605-2

DIMENSION BOOKS
Published by Bethany Fellowship, Inc.
6820 Auto Club Road, Minneapolis, Minnesota 55438

Printed in the United States of America

Dedication

To Dr. Oliver F. Bush—who has shown me how effectively personal affirmation fires the spark of creativity.

Phoebe Cranor is a Colorado cattle rancher's wife. She has nineteen years' experience as a Sunday school teacher and taught one year in the public school system in Arizona.

She is a graduate of Arizona State University, has had stories, poems and articles published and is presently active in an inner healing-prayer-counselling group, in church, and in writing. She is author of the best-selling book, *Why Did God Let Grandpa Die?*

Table of Contents

8

Preface

A carefully kept journal of any teaching experience is a journal of the education of the teacher. In the spiritual realm, especially, there is no possibility of the teacher "knowing the answers." Sometimes she is one step ahead of her pupils and sometimes they are one step ahead of her. The saving ingredient in the whole situation, though, is God's love, which permeates and fills and spills over a classroom where there is being conducted an honest search for Him. "Seek and you will find" is more true in the Sunday school class than anywhere else—IF we are really seeking. I have yet to see a "failure" among the pupils in a class where the group truly desired the presence of the living Lord.

One of my purposes in teaching, from the preschool group to these ever-different young Junior Highers, has always been to show each child that he is unique and lovely in the sight of his Maker. I can't do it by myself. Nobody on earth could

love and accept all of the children who pass
through the weekly roll call. It would be foolish
self-deception to pretend that I could. Some of
them simply rub me the wrong way. Some are
obnoxious to the point of no return. Some are
so insipid as to make even remembering that I
have seen them before difficult. I am imperfect,
too. Some Sundays I have nothing to give them
and we all know it. But Jesus can do what I can't.
The Holy Spirit can bring us into a consciousness
of His presence that overlooks and outweighs and
forgives me and my children's human inade-
quacies.

When Jesus told us to seek first the kingdom
of God and all the other things would be added,
He was giving a perfect formula for the success
of the integration of all these many diverse per-
sonalities into one weekly hour of joy. He was
telling us that if we wanted Him, He'd be there.
And I gradually began to trust Him. He solved
the problems that I couldn't even articulate. He
pieced together the brokenness and assembled the
jigsaw puzzle of our Sunday meetings in a way
that, even as I write it down, I have trouble believing. I didn't like "teaching" Junior High. But
I thoroughly enjoyed seeing what the Lord could
do when I turned it all over to Him. Why didn't
I always? Perhaps I should ask Him to tell me,
for I don't know the answer myself.

In any case, it is my hope that parents and
teachers and particularly the children themselves
will hear Him speaking to them in this record
of a period when I dealt with the middle-sized

children of the Junior High. Let Him use and revise my words to fit your situation. Let Him speak through you—with whatever help you can get from me. Each of us is uniquely blessed and as uniquely limited; but with Him there are no limits.

Chapter 1

Why Doesn't God Do Something?

"Why doesn't God do something? Why doesn't He just get busy and do something about it?"

What a way to begin the year with a group of seventh and eighth graders! If I had known that they were going to ask me that question, it is very unlikely that I would have ever agreed to be their leader. I had begun to experience the power and wisdom of the Holy Spirit shortly before, but I had not given Him complete consent to speak His words through my lips. I was a bit skeptical, still, that I could answer a question about which I had no knowledge and for which I had no answer. The day the intense little junior-high girl with a retarded sister broke through her shyness and dumped her feelings, I felt I had no reply for her.

How does one treat the pain of guilt, fear, loneliness, doubt and most of all anger and disappointment that come pouring from the mouth of a child? I sat listening—more and more in a panic as the other members of the class began to share their feelings. There was another retarded sibling in the group, and a deaf one. There was an alcoholic mother and an errant father. There was a secret bankruptcy. All at once, there was such a pile of hurt and anger that I felt like running. What could I say? How could I defend God—for that is what I felt I must do. It seemed to me that He was making something of a botch of the lives of these innocent children.

Suddenly I was angry. I was too angry to hide from myself the fact that I thought God had behaved in a very thoughtless and unloving way. Life is not fair. Why should these beautiful children have such hurts? "Original sin" was a pat reply that had no meaning; and the whole thing was an impossible mess. I knew that if I didn't have the answer for this elementary question, there would be no more Sunday school teaching for me. And perhaps there would be no more life. For what is life if at heart one is disillusioned with God? It was a moment of blackness. "Yea, though I walk through the valley of the shadow of death, I will fear no evil. . . ." I was in the valley of the shadow of death and I did fear. I feared death and all of the terrible implications; and I feared life just as much. It was a time of clarity such as Paul Tillich calls "the existential moment." I did not like such clarity. There was a long silence.

But then I remembered. Testing . . . testing

. . . would the Holy Spirit have an answer for me? It seemed impossible. But the children had exhausted their grief and were sitting, already embarrassed at having exposed so much of themselves. My image as a good teacher came to my rescue. I had to say SOMETHING. Oh, God. . . . Oh, God. . . . HELP!

Sure enough, as I made the step of opening my mouth, He poured in the words which have formed my philosophy of life ever since. He came to the edge of the abyss and held my hand, letting me look in, see, react, and then listen to His words. There is a plan. It is working. Let me cooperate, Lord.

For the Junior Highs

Supposing somebody told you that you had to write and direct a drama that had 900 billion people in it. Of course you are laughing. But suppose some more. Suppose that the drama had to have a point and an idea but nobody was required to learn lines or even know what the drama was all about. And besides all that, suppose that no matter what anyone did in the course of the drama, all the parts had to fit together to progress toward a final conclusion. You might as well give up. Nobody could do it. But, all the same, that is what God is doing.

Some people think that the world just happened and so did all of the people and animals and everything in it. But the people who think that can't explain some of the things that we can explain if we think of the big, big drama that we were just talking about. And lots of other people who are in the big drama—everybody is, whether he knows it or not—think God isn't caring a thing about them, even when they are praying to Him for all they are worth, because they don't see what the drama is about in the first place. They feel the way you'd feel if you were trying to watch a play with the curtains just drawn a tiny crack so you got only a peek at the stage. Nothing would make sense and you might think the play had no meaning at all. That would be because you could see only just such a wee bit. The drama God has going on is so big that it includes all the people who ever lived and who are ever going to live. When we said 900 billion, we were just making the number up. Nobody knows how many people there have been, and for sure nobody knows how many there are still going to be. And not very many people can understand how many even one billion really is.

Well then, what is the big drama all about? Shall we see if we can find out? Ever since the world began, there has been a plan for it. We can find little bits and pieces in all of the religions of the world. And we know that everyone, since time began, has had a place inside of him that wanted to be a part of the big plan. We know because when we find ruins of people so far back that they hadn't even learned to write, there are always things in them which show that the people worshipped God. Sometimes they worshipped lots of gods and sometimes they were afraid and did things to keep the gods from hurting them—they hoped. But the idea of God was always in the center of their lives somehow. Some of the things that are in our own Bible are in other religions, too. That is because God put those things into people's hearts.

Our own Bible, though, had God's big plan for His gigantic drama. It has all the acts and a star performer who was really the only one who ever completely understood the whole plan. You can guess who we are talking about, probably. But we aren't going to go into that just yet. We are going to talk about the first part of the drama. God began it with love. He made the whole world and the first people in it and gave them His love. The story of creation in Genesis makes the first creation of man and woman sound pretty special, doesn't it?

We can tell that God put love into people by watching small children who have come from homes where they are loved. They laugh and dance and sing and are so happy they make grown-ups laugh too. Love is natural, like hunger and thirst. God made it inside of us. But there are lots of other things besides love, and some-times they get in the way of it. Sometimes people are more interested in money or possessions or how famous they are or something else than they are in love. It has always been like that in the world. If we read the Bible from the beginning, we will see that people kept forgetting to be lov-ing; and whenever they forgot, they had troubles. Then God would send what was called a "prophet" to remind them that they had forgotten Him and

His love. Sometimes the people were sorry and turned back to Him and sometimes they didn't. If we are still thinking about the big drama, we can see that the people have always had the freedom to make up their own lines. God has seldom made anybody do anything that he didn't want to. And all through the Old Testament we can read of the people going off in their own way and getting themselves into trouble and then coming back to God again.

God kept sending prophets and holy men to tell people that the whole point of life was to love God, other people and themselves. They even put a little scroll on their doorposts which said, "You shall love the Lord your God with all your heart and all your mind and all your strength." Even then, though, the people forgot that the whole reason for their lives was to live love. They got busy doing things their own way and being more interested in something else than in God. He called that "worshipping false gods," and He was not happy with people who did it. The reason why was that God himself is love and when the people forgot one, they also forgot the other.

After a long while of trying to get the people to understand love by way of being good to them, sending prophets, telling them how to worship, God did something else. He sent the Star of our big drama to not just TELL people about love, but to show it to them in person. The Star, of course, was Jesus. He knew all about God being love and love being God because He himself was God. But He was also a person. He became a person, in fact, so that He could show people love. He did it in a lot of ways. He healed them when they were sick. He made them sane when they were insane. He straightened out their troubles and turned their focus again to love. He taught then what God is like and what He wants them to do. And, of course, He explained the whole idea of God's gigantic drama. He explained that God loves us so much that there is nothing He wants more than to have us live in total love all the time. Jesus died so we wouldn't be separated from God by anything.

Now we'll go back to the question that started all this discussion about the big drama: why doesn't God do something? Can you see from what we've already said, that when we get unhappy with God because we think He isn't doing anything, it is because we don't understand what He really is doing? He is always doing something. But sometimes it isn't what we have in mind that we'd like for Him to do. It is usually much bigger and more important. Remember that there are billions of people in the world and nobody is a puppet. God never makes people move to suit even Him, let alone you and me. The ways that He moves sometimes affect many more people than we think. But what He is doing, always and forever, is giving us chance after chance after chance to grow more loving—to grow more close to Him and to the Star of His drama: Jesus Christ. Jesus knows all about love and how to live it all the time. He sent the Holy Spirit to help us make contact with Him in every part of our lives.

So whenever we have things happen to us that we don't like and can't understand, we go to the Star of God's drama, by the power of the Holy Spirit, and say, "Jesus, please help me find a new way to love right now in the middle of this thing that has happened to me." Then we immediately see how this little scene in the drama can help us learn more about God's love.

We can talk to God and tell Him just how we feel and what we'd like and what we wish He would do. But if we were wise enough to direct a drama as big as He does, we might be terribly embarrassed to find out what a mess it would be if He did exactly what we asked Him to. The secret then? Talk everything over with God— exactly how you feel and what you want. Then stop and think about the big drama and the reason we are all here and say, "Father, how can I respond to this situation in my life with the same kind of love that Jesus does?" Wait a few minutes in quiet and see if you don't know inside yourself a good warm feeling that even though there are billions of people in the world, God has heard you and is doing something bigger than you would ever guess in answer to your prayer. Sometimes you see it the next day and sometimes you see it the next month. And maybe sometimes you never do see it. But after awhile, you begin to see that you are learning how to love. Then you know that you are doing what you were supposed to be doing in God's gigantic drama.

Even when you are worried about someone else, the same thing works. If you can ask Jesus how this particular situation helps develop love, then you will see that just your loving concern for someone else is causing good to happen. And if you are worried about drought or hurricane or some other natural happening, you can still see that out of each hard situation, there is a chance to learn more about loving. Sometimes we read about people who have been having a feud for years suddenly helping each other because of a storm or an earthquake. Maybe that is not the reason for a storm or an earthquake, but you might stop to wonder if anything else would have made those people friends again.

When we worry about people getting killed, we seem to be forgetting that God's love lasts on past death. The people who are killed in a natural disaster are just as much in God's love as they would be if they lived until the end of their lives and then died of old age. If your sister was killed and, in the experience, you learned a whole new approach to God's love. perhaps your sister is happy knowing that she is with Jesus and you are a more loving person. If we think of the bigness of the drama that we have been talking about, it helps us adjust to the things that happen when we know that we have a chance to go to a new spot in our journey toward love. We just have to keep asking the same question: how does this experience teach me more about God's love? Then God will show us and we will all be participating in the reason for our lives.

22

Scripture

Shout for joy, you heavens: exult, you earth!
You mountains, break into happy cries!
For Yahweh consoles his people
and takes pity on those who are afflicted.
—Isaiah 49:13

"*Can you not buy two sparrows for a penny?*
And yet not one falls to the ground without your
Father knowing. Why, every hair on your head
has been counted. So there is no need to be afraid;
you are worth more than hundreds of sparrows."
—Matthew 10:29:30

We know that by turning everything to their
good God cooperates with all those who love him,
and with all those that he has called according
to his purpose.—Romans 8:28

Chapter 2

Why Should Jesus Be the Only Way?

"My dad says one religion is as good as another." Tom's dad was a college professor, kindly
and knowledgeable. He never came to church,
but Tom was as regular as the calendar. His intense little face reflected his concern.

"My dad said it wouldn't be fair if only the
people that knew about Jesus got to heaven." The
other 12- and 13-year-olds nodded. Children in
those middle ages are frantically concerned with
"fair." It seemed unalterable to them that God
must be fair—by their standards. He must give
everyone an even chance and the same odds. I
have seen several children turn away from God
because He let the children of India starve or
the children of Japan die in an earthquake. My
students had listened and discussed the "big
drama" for two Sundays, and I felt that they had
made a start into the deeper walk of faith that
says, with Job, "Even though He slay me, still

I will trust Him." Growing in grace is a long slow process and can move at all only by God's gift of faith.

"Please," I begged the Lord, "please give these middle-sized children the gift of faith—of vision."

"What do you think would be fair?" I asked the boys and girls. "Things are different all over the world. Some people are healthy and some are crippled. Some are poor and some are rich. Some are cold and some are hot. What do you yourselves think of as 'fair'?" The children sat in silence. When children sit in silence, they are truly deliberating. Silence is uncommon country to them and in the moment before they began to speak, I knew my own time of panic. How would I ever be able to handle the discussion if I must explain God's plan? I needn't have worried. They shared their ideas for half an hour of heated discussion. And they got nowhere. There was no common definition of fairness that satisfied them. I stopped them just in time to keep the indecision from generating heat. I stopped them? No, the Holy Spirit stopped them.

"Listen," He seemed to be saying. "Let me tell you how it is." The children settled down and turned their attention to me. I opened my mouth, waiting, as I am learning to do, to see what the answer would be.

For the Junior Highs

Let's look at a mountain, to begin with. Let's think of the lower slopes that are grassy and not too steep. Think of people of all sizes and ages and colors climbing up the mountain. Some go pretty fast and some play along at their own pace. Some stop to take a nap. They can all look up and see the top of the mountain, more craggy and snowcapped: thoroughly shrouded with clouds. They can see that the higher they get up the mountain the harder it will be to climb, but from the lower slopes, they can't tell exactly what it will be like. There is a lot going on and everyone is having a great deal of fun. Some people are climbing in big groups and following a leader who is telling them what to do. Others are going along by themsleves. Some are having a picnic.

The rules for this climbing are quite simple, unless the people who are following a leader have the kind of leader who makes a lot of hard rules himself. The mountain doesn't make any hard rules. There are a few big streams but it is easy to avoid them by climbing up beside them or by finding stepping-stones on which to cross. The people are climbing all around the mountain. It doesn't make any difference what side they are on or where they stop, or for how long. They are all going up and up and up.

Finally, though, everyone gets up to the bottom of the high, craggy mountains. Here is a new situation. Suddenly the grass is gone and the easy slopes are done. The high mountains are harder to climb. If the people want to go on up, they must quit playing around and get down to business. They must really work.

Many people do work and many of them get up the high mountains. Most of them are happy and satisfied. But some of them aren't. They have come to a new part of the mountain. It is impossible to climb. It is separated from the very top by a deep, straight-edged chasm which there seems to be absolutely no way to cross. They walk all around the mountain looking for a way to get over the chasm, because they have the urge to get to the very absolute top of the mountain. (There are many mountains all over the world that challenge professional mountain climbers and there are a few that have been climbed only once or twice all told.)

Now when the few climbers who are really determined to get to the absolute top of the mountain get almost all the way around the chasm, they suddenly discover a tiny, narrow bridge. It looks dangerous and precarious, but it is the only way there exists to cross. They must cross right there, on that one bridge or not at all. Fog is everywhere. There is no choice. They have to make the decision as they stand there by the bridge. "Do I climb to the top of the mountain, or don't I?" If they decide to go, then they must walk across the bridge. If they decide not to cross the bridge, then they have decided that they are not going to climb to the top. Even if they think they will go rent a helicopter and drop on the top of the mountain, they are mistaken, because the top is so shrouded in clouds that it isn't possible to approach it by any other method.

Now we aren't lost from what we were talking

about at all. We are discussing the way life really is. There are lots of things that are very general and can be done any number of ways. I might fold the napkins for dinner in a square or in a long rectangle. I might ride my bicycle on the grass or on the sidewalk or on the sand or in the rocks. I can't, however, ride it on the water. I might ski on snow or sand or water or maybe even on grass. But I can't ski on rocks. I can sail a boat on water but it doesn't do too well in the meadow. Certain limitations just do exist everywhere. Even in math they do. If you have a bag of apples there is only one way you can count them and get the right number of apples.

All the other religions are like the lower part of the mountain. They move up toward the top where God is. He can see the people all over the mountain and they can talk to Him and hear Him. There is no one religion that gets people up the grassy part of the mountain any better than another. Some religions stop as soon as the going gets a little bit tough. They take the people only part way toward God. Some religious leaders make hard rules to follow and make the journey very difficult. That is not God's fault. It is the fault of the leaders. Some leaders make the whole thing one big picnic, too, and some people have a big picnic all the way up the easy part. They probably don't even want to get any closer to God than the grassy slopes of the mountain.

But God himself is at the very top of the mountain. He has given us the Bible to explain to us that He is love, that He loves us and that He wants us to give ourselves in love to each other and to Him. That is a difficult thing to do. We are separated from Him by a big chasm. The chasm is the hard time we have living love. It is called sin, which is another name for the division between us and God caused by the fact that we don't always like love or want to live it.

Jesus Christ is, as you know, God himself made into a person so He can show us what God is like. Jesus Christ is the only person in all of the religions who is totally free of sin and totally able to live love all the time. He is the bridge between us and God. The way is very narrow. It is just like the runway for an airplane—it is narrow so you can get the plane exactly where it needs to be. Jesus is the only religious figure who explains to us that God is our Father and loves us; that we are all brothers with Jesus for a big brother; that God has created us to participate with Him in love and that we can't live love by ourselves without help. That is the top of the mountain. The clouds keep us from seeing just exactly what it is like to live in perfect love all the time. Jesus told us, "I am the way, the truth, and the life and nobody comes to the Father except through me." He meant that He is the only bridge across the chasm at the top of the mountain. He is the only way we can really reach God himself in person across the big chasm which is separating us. That is because Jesus himself is love.

Do you see how it is true that all religions do lead to God and at the same time it is true that Christianity is the only way? The others all lead us toward God. But Jesus is the bridge that lets us get to God.

Heaven is on top of the mountain with God. Heaven is never, ever being separated from love. The people who want to live in total love for all the time, and even after time is not a fact any more, have to get on up the mountain. The grassy slopes are nice, but they are not the same as love. They have a lot of distractions, pain, and sadness. Love is perfect. We probably don't get to see all the way what perfect love is until we go up into the part that still looks all cloudy—until we have climbed a few more years and it is time for us to die in these bodies and live in new, perfect ones. But if we have crossed the bridge that leads us *to* God, then we know we are safe in love all the rest of eternity.

These are the reasons why the people who know Jesus insist that He is the only way. It may not seem fair that there are people living down the side of the mountain who never get high enough to find the little bridge. It may not seem fair that they haven't heard about it. It isn't fair, in our eyes, that some people are born crippled or retarded, either, but God has solved all those problems. He may have some plan to help the people who haven't heard about Jesus get to the bridge *after* they die. We just don't know that. But the thing that is a great big puzzle to the people who know and love Jesus is why some people refuse to cross the bridge that they do know is there just because not everyone has found it. If you found a beautiful ripe strawberry hiding in the woods, you wouldn't refuse to eat it just because not everyone else had found it, would you? Or if you came to a big Thanksgiving dinner, you wouldn't sit without eating just because the children in Japan didn't have anything but fish.

One of God's plans is that we live the best way we know right where we are. We can tell everyone that we know about Jesus and love Him ourselves and take His hand to cross the chasm so we can reach God. Then we can leave the rest of the people on the mountain to God to take care of. We can let *Him* worry about the fairness of His plan.

Scripture

"Yahweh your God will circumcise your heart and the heart of your descendants, until you love Yahweh your God with all your heart and soul, and so have life."—Deuteronomy 30:6

I knew you then only by hearsay; but now, having seen you with my own eyes, I retract all I have said, and in dust and ashes I repent.—Job 42:5-6

On this mountain he will remove the mourning veil covering all peoples, and the shroud enwrapping all nations, he will destroy Death for ever. The Lord Yahweh will wipe away the tears from every cheek; he will take away his people's shame everywhere on earth, for Yahweh has said so. That day, it will be said: See, this is our God in whom we hoped for salvation; Yahweh is the one in whom we hoped. We exult and we rejoice that he has saved us; for the hand of Yahweh rests on this mountain.—Isaiah 25:8-11

"I am the Way, the Truth, and the Life. No one can come to the Father except through me. If you know me, you know my Father too. From this moment you know him and have seen him."
—John 14:6-8

For there is only one God, and there is only one mediator between God and mankind, himself a man, Christ Jesus, who sacrificed himself as a ransom for them all.—1 Timothy 2:5-6

Chapter 3

Can I Commit an Unpardonable Sin?

I, too, used to be a worrier. I still feel the chill of waking up in the night worrying about a thunderstorm or rabies or some other, to me at the time, awful calamity. I was afraid of stepping on a nail or of displeasing my mother or of offending my neighbor. And I am grateful to God that He protected me from finding out that there was mentioned in His Holy Word anything about an unpardonable sin. I would probably have died of worry for fear I would commit it unaware. So I was very much tuned with an inner understanding to the problem of the little visitor that one of my Junior Highs brought to class one Sunday.

She was a funny little country cousin who refused to go to the class for nine-year-olds. As soon as I looked into her eyes I knew that she had a problem which made her old beyond her years. Hardly waiting for the class to begin, she looked defiantly at me and burst out with her torment.

"I hate God!"

"Why do you hate Him?" I asked. She erupted into a torrent of tears and threw herself into my lap with all the force of her desperation.

People say that children are cruel. Perhaps they are. I have always found that although they are often ignorant and fearful—they are, underneath, tender and compassionate. My group of junior high boys and girls saw this little girl's need and, fearful or not, they responded with true gentleness. They left off all of their nonsense and sat patiently while she tried to regain her composure. It was a moment of confrontation with Him who said, "Let the children come to me." There He was. We felt Him; we knew Him; we reached out to Him.

Amid sobs and snuffles Patty's story emerged. Some thoughtless adult had told her that she could, without knowing it, commit some sin so great that she would be forever separated from God. But what the sin was, nobody seemed to be able to tell her. She had finally given up under the strain of always searching her behavior to make sure she wasn't doing it—whatever it might be—and had decided that a god so enigmatic and cruel was not worthy of her love. Yet the fear that she might live forever in hell because of her decision and her actions still hung over her. It was a burden too great for anyone of any age. Lord, where did this awful thing come from and what can we do?

We sat still for a long moment waiting for Patty to control herself. As we did, I saw that her inner turmoil existed in the hearts of the older children as well. And in mine? I knew with a flash of holy light that most of us are afraid we can do something so awful that God will discard us. The legalists who refuse to look past the Bible-Rule-Book which they carry in their heads are afraid in much the same way. The compulsives who live in fear of omens; the horoscope addicts, these all have a common lack of faith in a consistently loving God. "Many are called but few are chosen"; "all who are destined for eternal life became believers." These sound as if God doesn't want us all and has made provision to eliminate some just out of the hardness of His heart. Will I be eliminated? Patty's insecurity lies in the hearts of all of us in one way or another.

And yet, He died to save us. He was and is infallibly compassionate, understanding, and forgiving. Seventy times seven is, in reality, an unending number. Holy Spirit, help me speak to Patty and to the junior highs and to all of us with what I need to know myself: my Father loves me and wants me forever and ever.

I spoke in the language of a fourth grader, but the eyes of the bigger children never left my face.

For the Children

Supposing your mother is making cookies. They look so good that you reach for one before she gets them off the pan. She says to you, "Be careful! You'll burn yourself if you touch those cookies." And sure enough, if you go ahead and pick one up you'll burn your hand and if you stick it quick into your mouth, you'll burn your tongue. Was that your mother's mean old rule? Would you be mad at your mother for making such a cruel rule? Of course you wouldn't. You know it wasn't your mother's rule that cookies will burn you. It was a fact that she was warning you about. You can think of lots of other things like that. If you play with a razor blade, you'll cut your fingers. If you spill ink on your clothes, your clothes will be blue or black or whatever color the ink is. Those are just things that are true. If someone tells you about them, you know the person is just telling you a fact and not making up a rule. So you don't blame the person for the thing that he told you.

Now God made a lot of rules that are important to keep the world running smoothly. One rule is called gravity. You know what it does. It makes whatever weighs anything fall to the ground. That is an important rule to keep the trees and houses and people from flying off into space. But it is also the rule that makes you land hard on the sidewalk when you fall out of a tree. The rule isn't bad, but if you do certain things the rule will be the cause of your getting hurt—like falling out of the swing.

In the Bible God tells us some of the things He has planned and why, and He also tells us what will happen to us if we make a mistake and don't follow the rules He has made. For example, a long time ago God told the people that there were certain kinds of meat that would make them sick. He wasn't saying that they were bad if they ate the meat and He would punish them for it. He just gave the fact that the meat would make them sick. That was nice of Him. It was kind of Him to warn them, just as it was kind of your mother to warn you not to burn your hand on the hot cooky.

Now one of the things God did was to tell the people that there was a way they could get so far away from Him that they could never find their way back again. This is how it works.

Pretend there is a boy in your block who wants to be friends with you. Every time he sees you, he speaks to you and he seems to go out of his way to be where you are and to say hello. But you don't care to be friends with him. You don't answer or pay any attention to him. Still he keeps trying to get you to notice him. Finally he brings you a present and then another present. Instead of taking his presents, you go on acting as if he weren't even there. You don't look at him or speak to him and if anybody mentions him to you, you say, "There's no such boy. He isn't real." You keep on doing that for awhile but the boy keeps on being there. Finally you start walking away. You walk and walk, faster and faster until finally you have walked so far that you have gotten away from him. Now you are clear into another town and he is no longer around. You have gotten rid of him. He has quit being there and speaking to you or bringing you presents.

If somebody told you, the way your mother told you that the cookies would burn you, that you would get rid of the boy by pretending he wasn't there and walking away from him, you would not think much about it. You wouldn't say that was a bad rule. You would say that he had told you the truth. That is what God has done: He has told you the truth.

If you ignore the Holy Spirit and keep acting as if He weren't there, you will hurt His feelings, just as you would probably have hurt the boy's feelings that we were talking about before. You can keep on hurting His feelings and walking away from Him, no matter how nice He is to you or what kind of presents He gives you, until you finally get so far away that He quits trying to get you to notice Him any more. Since the Holy Spirit is part of God, you are putting yourself a long way from God. And where is hell? It is away from God. You have walked and walked away from God until you are as far from Him as you can get. He warned us that if we keep saying and acting as if He isn't real, we will be moving away from Him. That's just a fact, like "cookies out of the oven are hot."

Nobody can make a mistake and walk away from God by accident. A person who worries even the tiniest little bit about getting away from God won't, because he isn't pretending that God isn't real or that all the good things God has done for us are just an accident. We can be mad at God and He will forgive us because He made us and He understands how we feel. He will love us and forgive us if we don't want to have anything to do with Him, too, but we won't know it or care about it. What good does it do you to have somebody love you if you don't even believe he is alive? Now if you are afraid that you will do something so bad that God won't love you any more or if you are afraid that He hasn't chosen you and you are left out in the cold, remember that He chose everybody. He loves everybody and wants everybody to love Him, too. He is like a person choosing up teams. He says, "I choose you and you and you" to everybody He ever made. But if somebody says, "I won't play," then God won't make him. He lets us decide whether we will walk away from Him or not, but if you care even a little bit what He thinks of you, you can be sure you are safe. He knows that you don't want to make any mistakes and He will watch you and keep you from getting lost. And He will give you love gifts and make you happy, besides, because you are so special.

Scripture

What! Am I likely to take pleasure in the death of a wicked man—it is the Lord Yahweh who speaks—and not prefer to see him renounce his wickedness and live?—Ezekiel 18:23

I am the Holy One in your midst and have no wish to destroy.—Hosea 11:9B

But there is one thing, my friends, that you must never forget: that with the Lord, "a day" can mean a thousand years and a thousand years *is like a day. The Lord is not being slow to carry out his promises, as anybody else might be called slow; but he is being patient with you all, wanting nobody to be lost and everybody to be brought to change his ways.* —2 Peter 3:8-9

Chapter 4

What Will Happen If I Get Mad at God?

Nationally we are becoming more aware of the need to recognize and deal with negative feelings. Many people go to psychiatrists and receive help in acknowledging and understanding all of their emotions. But there is still a thread left over from the past which says that we mustn't (and don't dare) be angry at God. I know about it very well. I grew up with an older, very old-fashioned mother who said with regularity, "Nice girls don't feel that way. Nice girls don't say things like that. Nice girls control their emotions."

And of course I had to be a "nice girl," didn't I? So I suppressed and repressed and hid my feelings. If God happened to be like my mother, He would probably spank me if I let Him know that I was angry at Him. Somewhere inside, I felt that as long as I didn't know it myself, He could also be kept from finding out. Such a situation is charged with potential ulcers, at the very least.

A good deal of the same kind of inner deception must have been prevalent in the lives of my Junior Highers. They could honestly and fearlessly tell me, their teacher, that I had made them angry. They could certainly tell each other. But God? That presented another problem altogether. The week before they had been silent and compassionate with their little visitor. They had concentrated on her distress and their feelings of love and empathy for her. All of a sudden the idea hit them: What will God do to Patty for saying that she hated Him? And underneath their concern was the incoming awareness that she was not the only one. Somewhere inside each one, I am sure, was a little thread of hate and anger that Patty's outburst had made it impossible to deny. They were really desperate. They had left off their usual blasé nonsense and become frightened children, clinging to their teacher for comfort.

And sure enough, their teacher had also seen her own anger and heard the old voice from the past saying, "Nice girls don't . . ." All right, Lord, we're not nice children. We're bad and hopeless. What are you going to do about us? Here we are, confronted with our own feelings and we have no place to hide. Your compassion is all we have to count on. Help us, please.

For the Junior Highs

Supposing that you had three moles on your

body. One was on each shoulder and one in the middle of your back. You hated them and didn't want anyone to know they were there. You never went swimming or wore backless outfits because you were so anxious for nobody to see them. Wearing your clothes, of course, kept you from even thinking about the moles, so you were pretty happy most of the time. But then, suppose you had to have a physical exam or something and you had to take off all of your clothes and stand in the bright light. You have only two hands, so you couldn't cover all three of the moles at once. You would have to let go and let the doctor or whoever was examining you see the moles, wouldn't you? There they'd be, all exposed and out in the open.

Then, suppose the doctor looked at the moles and said casually, "Those aren't anything. They are just part of your natural pigment. Most people have them somewhere or other. Instead of trying to hide them, why not just accept them as a natural part of yourself?" Wouldn't you be relieved? Wouldn't you be glad he'd seen them and reassured you? Perhaps it had never crossed your mind that most people have moles and that nobody would think much about it if you did let them show.

Jesus told us that He is the "light of the world." He said that men who like darkness and have darkness inside of them don't like light. That makes sense. But what kind of "light" do you think Jesus meant? He didn't mean just the kind of light that shines in the bedroom while you get ready for bed. He meant a kind of light that shines inside you and shows up all the deep dark secrets that you think are hidden away from God. It is very easy for us to keep a secret from ourselves. I can pretend that I don't feel angry at God, for example, so carefully that I fool myself. I have kept a secret from myself.

But you know, I have *not* kept a secret from God. He is the light that shines into all darkness. He can see inside of me and He knows my secret because He made me. Everything that is inside of me is clear to Him. He made me exactly the way I am, too, with or without three moles.

As soon as the light is turned on and we can see whatever is inside ourselves, then we realize that God knows too: that He knew before we did. That changes all of our feelings. Last week little Patty said, "I hate God." She knew how she felt and she said it. She wasn't hiding it from herself. But she and all the rest of us wondered what God would do if she said it out loud. If all of the inside of Patty were filled with light and nothing was hidden from God, then He must have known that she was mad at Him even before she said it—or whether she said it or didn't say it.

When God made us, He decided how we were to be constructed and He constructed us that way. He wanted us to have lots of feelings. He wanted us to have anger as well as joy. Those feelings are part of what makes us people and when God made them, He knew that He had use for them. Remember that Jesus was angry with the people

44

who had made the courtyard of the temple into
a market? He was angry at wickedness and sel-
fishness. And He was God himself in the flesh.
If we try to hide away feelings of anger, we are
trying to hide a part of ourselves which God
wanted us to have.

But feelings are just like anything else. We
have control of how we are going to use them.
You have hands and you could do many wicked
things with them. Or you could do many helpful
things with them. You have brains and you are
free to use them for thinking of things that are
destructive or things that are constructive. You
have anger and you can either use it to do good
or you can let it get the best of you and do bad.
And everyone of us has that choice. It is our own
choice.

God made everyone with lots of feelings and
talents and ideas. He sent Jesus as His bright
light to show on everything we have. God loves
us and His love created us. His love is the bright
light. That means that when someone says "I
am mad at God," the bright light of God's love
shines on that "mad." Bright light helps us to
see what the "mad" is caused by and what we
can do with it. God's love does not hate the mad.
He understands and doesn't condemn it at all.
Sometimes WE condemn it. But God doesn't.
He shines His light—Jesus—on it and then we
understand and get right to work to use it for what
it was meant to be used.

What was little Patty's "mad" good for?
Think how badly she wanted to be free of fear

and feel safe with God. Her being so mad that she got over being shy was what let her tell us her trouble and ask for help. The "mad" was like a big bulldozer pushing away shyness and letting her get to the point of feeling more loving toward God. God can deal with anything that is inside of us, even the things we ourselves think are the worst. He sent the Holy Spirit to shine bright light into every corner—if we will let Him.

Now let's "suppose." Let's suppose that you have a closet in the back corner of your bedroom. Inside this closet, you have boxes and boxes of things that you don't like. You have hurt feelings and anger and jealousy and greediness. You don't want your friends or your parents or your teachers to see these things, which is why you have them in the secret closet to begin with. And somehow, just because nobody else is allowed to see all those unpleasant looking things, you feel that God can't see them either. Of course that isn't true. He knows they are there. But He is and always has been a gentleman. He won't yank open the door and show the world that you have ugly secrets in your back bedroom closet. Still, because you have the door shut and you don't think about them any oftener than you can help it, the ugly secrets stay pretty much the same all the time.

That's where the bright light comes in. If you can bring your uglinesses out in the open and show them to God, He will let you see what they are really for. He will let you see that maybe they aren't ugly at all, but are characteristics that you

46

need to do and be what He created you for. He will shine light on them and let you know that, like the three moles we were talking about before, these are just natural characteristics that are part of the way you were made. Then He will show you how to use those characteristics to be a more whole person. He is pleased with you when you let Him into every part of your life. Don't complicate your life by hiding part of yourself from yourself. God will help you grow to be whatever is best for you if you open all your doors to Him.

Scripture

Yahweh, you examine me and know me, you know if I am standing or sitting, you read my thoughts from far away; whether I walk or lie down, you are watching, you know every detail of my conduct. . . . Where could I go to escape your spirit? Where could I flee from you presence? . . . You know me through and through, from having watched my bones take shape when I was being formed in secret, knitted together in the limbo of the womb.—Psalm 139:1-2, 7, 15

Long before they call I shall answer; before they stop speaking I shall have heard.—Isaiah 65:24

It is never the will of your Father in heaven that one of these little ones should be lost.—Matthew 18:14

". . . for the Son of Man has come to seek out and save what was lost."—Luke 19:10

We are God's work of art, created im Christ Jesus to live the good life as from the beginning he had meant us to live it.—Ephesians 2:10

Chapter 5

What Are Miracles?

One of the older men of the church had taken it upon himself to prove that there have never been miracles. Starting with the first miracle in the Bible, he had systematically dealt with them, trying to form scientific explanations that would pacify his fear of the supernatural. Perhaps he had succeeded to his own satisfaction, but many of the people to whom he delivered his "teachings" were far from comfortable. In the long run, I know that the work he did was used by our faithful Lord to bring forth fruits in the lives of his friends.

In the meantime, though, my Junior High group had become involved. They were hotly discussing the lectures that they had heard about from their parents—repeating and restating and arguing. And modern children do know so much! They see events and concepts on television that their elders had no idea existed when they were young. Their minds are stretched and bombarded

and confused. Their world is full of miracles.
How can one go about demythologizing them
when the cowboy heroes die before their eyes one
day and are going strong again the next? These
cartoon friends, whom they have known all their
lives, are continually being flattened paper-thin
and twisted into corkscrews only to revive in the
next scene for more mischief. Middle-sized children have barely, if at all, stepped out of the
fantasy world where Peter Rabbit and Jesus
Christ are equally existent or nonexistent. The
Holy Spirit and the green ghost must compete,
and the artist's rendition of the ghost comes out
far ahead. When I taught kindergarten, I spent
many class periods helping my little people decide which concept was "real" and which was
"pretend."

Besides their closeness to the acceptance
which is characteristic of small children, Junior
Highers are still emotionally geared to miracles
—to love and magic and dreams-come-true. The
reason they aren't as impressed with, for example, the Easter story as we wish they were,
is that it all seems so right to them. After all,
Jesus was the "good guy." Of course poetic justice would revive Him. He would naturally be
just like any good story-cartoon character and
return because He was the star of the show.

And isn't that the way God meant it to be?
Surely He put into us the urge for good to triumph
over evil; for right to prevail. Even in the oldest
myths, the resurrection story is foretold. And in
the grown-ups' hearts, if they have been protected

the least bit from an inundation of sin, lies forever the hope that we will not only NOT vanish into nothingness but will get to go on and finish the good works that we are doing, besides. Scripture bears this hope out. When we discover that, it is like a great sigh of relief and joy.

Could there be a ground for their understanding of miracles that would satisfy both my children's will-indoctrinated "scientific approach" and their natural bent toward the supernatural? If there could, only the Lord himself could produce it. Lord, will you—again—give us the miracle of understanding for the children?

For the Children

Have you ever taken a magnifying glass outside into the sunshine and turned it until you got the rays focused into such a bright spot of light that it set something on fire? Have you ever moved it along, making "writing" on a board or a paper with the burned spots? There is no more heat in the sunshine before you hold your glass in it than there is afterward. The glass just gathers the rays together and focuses them in one spot.

Love is everywhere, even more than the sunshine is. Just as sunshine makes plants grow, so love makes everything grow. God created our bodies so that when they are hurt, they will repair themselves and get well. Most of us know that people who are hurt or sick do not get well nearly as fast if they do not feel loved. Sometimes, in fact, they do no get well at all. That is, of course, not the only thing that causes people to die. But experiments with babies in orphan homes have shown us that they will either die or be retarded if they never receive love.

If the absence of love will cause people *not* to get well, then we may assume that the presence of love helps them to heal. If we think hard about the magnifying glass, we will see that if love could be concentrated in one spot the way sunshine was, it would be very powerful. If a little love could help our bodies get well more quickly, then perhaps a big concentration of love in one spot, as if with a giant magnifying glass, would really speed the process up.

That is exactly what God did for us about two thousand years ago! He concentrated love into one spot over in Bethlehem one winter night and made it like a giant magnifying glass: Jesus. As Jesus grew, we might say He kept turning the glass around and around until when He was grown he got it just right to concentrate love into one very bright spot. And then what happened? He touched people and instead of taking days or weeks or months to get well, they were healed right then. The concentration of love speeded things up just as the concentration of the sun's rays in one place by the magnifying glass got a spot so hot it burst into flames. A miracle is not something that is out of step with science. It always fits into the general pattern, but it is the concentration of love that brings all of the forces together in just the right way to cause the miracles to come to pass.

God focused His love in one spot several times before Jesus came to be a man here on earth. There are places in the Bible where someone else was used as an instrument, as the magnifying glass was used, in concentrating power in one spot. Read in your Bible about the Israelites crossing the Red Sea or Moses striking a rock and water coming or about the manna from heaven. These were all miracles caused by a surge of love from God coming through loyal, loving men who really cared for, not only God, but His people. When Jesus came, it was different. Jesus was not just a man, like Abraham and Moses. He was God himself also. He was not just love being focused by God from a distance. He was both the sunshine and the magnifying glass at the same time. That made Him a really potent force of love. There was nothing He couldn't do with so much love. He could turn water into wine instantly instead of waiting for the grapes to be added and ferment as is usually done. He could make people well just by touching them, even people who were so ill that they could never get well on their own. He could cure insanity and epilepsy and cast out any evil thing of darkness that existed. He could turn a few fishes into enough food for a crowd.

Love can even reverse processes that are started. If you have been getting madder and madder or sadder and sadder and someone comes and gives you some real loving understanding, then the processes reverse themselves. You get over being mad or sad and become happy.

Love has done it. If your mood was reversed by love, then how about your sickness? If you are very sick and you feel a great surge of love, such as Jesus gives, you begin to recover. This is the thing that happened when Jesus reversed Lazarus from dead and decaying to being alive again. He did to him the same thing that He does to destructive forces anywhere: He counteracted them with love. He turned death around and made it life again just by concentrating such a surge of love into the situation.

When Jesus himself died on the cross, it was a very important miracle. Jesus had taken all of the sin, evil and ugliness of the world onto himself, and, like the lamb in the Jews' ancient sacrifice, He had to shed His blood to get rid of all that stuff. That meant that, to reverse all the evil, He had to have a terrific amount of concentrated love flow through Him. It was an important moment in history, because if He couldn't reverse all of the evil in the world and defeat it, then it would eventually have the upper hand. He had to focus the love so strong in one spot that He burned everything to a crisp except the love itself. He had to take all of the worst there was to take: being hated and deserted and hurt and scorned even by His best friends and finally die in the worst way there was to die in order that, when the concentration of love came, it would burn up all the bad that He had taken onto himself at once.

Jesus didn't put an end to wickedness in the world. There is still a lot of it around. But He did one thing that will eventually mean the end of evil. He proved that love is stronger than any kind of badness there is anywhere. Love can defeat evil and death and decay—as well as sadness and madness and meanness. We can hold our difficulties up to Jesus, who is love, and just like sunshine focused through a magnifying glass, that love will turn them into good. It won't always make them go away instantly, as we would like it to, though. What it will do, instead, is turn them into something that is centered in love.

Miracles aren't over. They still happen all the time. Love causes all kinds of miracles, and we must be always ready to notice one when it happens. And we can help them along by letting the love of God flow through us. We can decide to be little magnifying glasses and let God's love focus in us, too. Then we can be part of God's miracles.

Scripture

A leper now came up and bowed low in front of him. "Sir," he said, "if you want to, you can cure me." Jesus stretched out his hand, touched him and said, "Of course I want to! Be cured!" And his leprosy was cured at once.—Matthew 8:1-5

Jesus said to him, "Receive your sight. Your faith has saved you." And instantly his sight returned and he followed him praising God.— Luke 18:41

That evening they brought him many who were possessed by devils. He cast out the spirits with a word and cured all who were sick.—Matthew 8:16-17

Still sighing, Jesus reached the tomb: it was a cave with a stone to close the opening. Jesus said, "Take the stone away." Martha said to him, "Lord, by now he will smell; this is the fourth day." Jesus replied, "Have I not told you that if you believe you will see the glory of God?" So they took away the stone.... "Lazarus, here! Come out!" The dead man came out.... —John 11:39-41 and 43

In the evening of that same day, the first day of the week, the doors were closed in the room where the disciples were, for fear of the Jews. Jesus came and stood among them. He said to them, "Peace be with you," and showed them his hands and his side. The disciples were filled with joy when they saw the Lord and he said to them again, "Peace be with you."—John 20: 19-21

Chapter 6

Why Doesn't God Make Me Good?

Art was one of the kind of seventh graders that make teachers wish they had gone into any other career instead of education. He never stopped talking and he had a most uncanny talent for finding out what someone didn't want him to do and then doing it. Besides he was funny. That was the worst part. He could snap up the attention of the rest of the class in a flash with his wit. In other words, Art was a pain. But for some reason, I loved him. I loved him so much that sometimes I wondered what had happened to my common sense. He was forever disrupting my class and I often sent him to sit on a bench outside so that we could finish something important. Still, there was a breath of the Spirit about his humor and his creativeness; and he loved me, too. And with the same talent that showed him how to do whatever people *didn't* want him to, he could also see what someone needed most.

Sometimes his sensitivity was overwhelming. In a time of real trouble, Art could be a mainstay.

One day this funny big child stayed after class. He lingered. He puttered. I knew he had something on his mind and I knew I would have to wait until everything was right before he would tell me. So I set out to clean my closet, waiting while seeming not to wait for him to unburden his heart.

"Lord," I prayed, "send your Spirit into Art and into me and into this place, and let this boy out of his prison—whatever it is." After a bit, he sat down on a pile of books, looked up at me and said, his voice shaking, "I wish God would just make me good. It makes me mad that He doesn't just make me do what He wants me to instead of always letting me be in trouble. It's no fair. I can't help the way I am." His eyes were bright with tears a boy his age felt no freedom to shed. I had to be very careful not to upset his control, not to preach, not to offend. I had been given the gift of his confidence and I treasured it with care.

"Help," I prayed again. "Please, please give me the words for Art—and for all of us," for I knew a great surge of kinship with this boy in his distress.

The Junior High spring party was coming up. All of the youngsters had been discussing it, and I had seen Art's enthusiasm about the event. "Start there," I seemed to be hearing. So I took a deep breath, pulled up a box and began, watching Art's face as I talked, for the lift I knew he needed.

For the Children

Think with me for a minute about a very special party coming up right away. Think of the decorations and the favors and the games. Think of the girls' pretty dresses and how their hair will look and how they will smell. Think of the boys all dressed up and looking their best. Think of the good refreshments. The party is a very special event. Now think of the girls. You have a girl you like better than the rest. And if you were a girl, you would have a boy all picked out that you would rather go with than anyone else. That's part of what makes the spring party so special. Taking the nicest girl to the most perfect event is like putting a lovely present into an elegant gift-wrap and handing it to someone you care especially for.

Let's go on with this by thinking about the girl herself. You know her from class all year. You know that she is pretty and popular and sometimes funny and sometimes sad. Sometimes she's even mean. You don't care. You like her just the way she is. But you're not entirely sure how well she likes you. Sometimes you catch her watching you and you think maybe she really does like you. Other times she's busy with some other fellow and you are not at all sure she even knows you're around. That makes you worry. Will she go to the party with you or will she go with someone else? You get to work trying to win her favor. You carry her books and help her with her math. You walk her home. You buy her pop or an ice cream cone. You take extra showers, wash your hair, even wear a new sweater you think makes you look good.

One day you catch her in the hall and you take a deep breath and ask her to the party. Your knees are shaking and your voice comes out a little bubbly for fear she'll say "no," and you'll be terribly disappointed. But she doesn't say "no." She gives you a big smile and says, "Yes, I'd love to." You feel like jumping and clapping your hands (although, of course you don't do it). You have won her favor over the rest of the guys. For the moment, she is "your girl." You feel special and tall and particularly lucky.

All right now, we have one more little pretend to do. Suppose the girl doesn't say "yes," at all. She says "no." But suppose there is another girl that you know you can ask. You don't particularly care for her, so you were hoping you wouldn't have to ask her. You don't care for her because she is not interesting; the reason why she is not interesting is because she is a puppet. She has strings on her and little buttons, so all you have to do to get her to do *exactly* what you want her to, is pull a string or push a button. You can get her to sing or sit down or tell you you are handsome. You can make her every move for her, just by pressing or pulling. So how much fun is that? You know that you haven't won her away from the other boys. You know that she will never do anything on her own at all. There is no waiting and wondering whether or not she will go to the party with you. If you push the "go" button, she will go and she will play all the games. But you don't want her. You want a girl who can choose anyone in the school to go with and she chooses *you*. That makes you special and her special and the party special.

God gave everyone brains and personality, all different. He gave us the power to make decisions. He gave us the freedom to do things just as we like, exactly, to think out what we want and try to get it. God did that for just the same reason that you would give your girl the freedom to be herself—even if it meant saying "no" when you asked her to the party. If your girl has the freedom to say whatever she wants, and she decides to say "yes" to you because she likes you and wants to go with you, then you feel you have something of value. She could have said "no," and she didn't, so her "yes" really means something. It means, "I am going to the party with you *because I want to*." That is what makes you clap your hands with joy.

The reason God does not just make you good is the same reason that you do not want your girl to be a puppet. He wants you to bring the personality that He has given you, just as it is, to Him and say, "God, I want to team up with *you*. I want to go through life with you because I have decided I like you." That decision is worth something.

There are millions of people in the world— billions since mankind began. Every one is different. God made each person unique because He wanted each person just as he is to complete His kingdom. You would not like a puppet girl who only did what you wanted her to do and God would not like a puppet any better. What He wants is for you, just as you are (which *He* made), to choose Him. That is much better than having Him make you exactly as you yourself or your parents or your teachers or your friends want you to be. It is even better than having God himself turn you into a puppet.

I can just hear you wondering how I know what God wants. Well, I'll tell you how I know. God made us in His own image. The book of Genesis in the Bible tells us that. Being made like God, we can tell how He feels by how we feel. God is perfect and holy and we never feel *exactly* as He does, of course. But still, we have the same things in us that He has in himself, like love and loyalty and creativity, and others that you can think of yourself. Puppets are not creative. You like people who do things on their own, even at the risk that they will do things you don't like. So, I think we can assume that God is like that, too. He endowed us with all kinds of freedom and let us have the ability to have all kinds of ideas. That is so that when we choose *Him* it is special, just like when the girl you like best of all chooses you. That is a time for celebration!

Scripture
Moses then went up to God, and Yahweh called to him from the mountain, saying, "Say this to the House of Jacob, declare this to the sons of Israel, 'You yourselves have seen what I did with the Egyptians, how I carried you on eagle's wings and brought you to myself. From this you know

62

*that now, if you obey my voice and hold fast to
my covenant, you of all the nations shall be my
very own, for all the earth is mine. I will count
you a kingdom of priests, a consecrated nation.'
Those are the words you are to speak to the sons
of Israel." So Moses went and summoned the elders of the people, putting before them all that
Yahweh had bidden him. Then all the people answered as one, "All that Yahweh has said, we
will do." And Moses took the people's reply back
to Yahweh.—Exodus 19:3-9*

*Ahaz was twenty years old when he came to
the throne and he reigned for sixteen years in
Jerusalem. He did not do what is pleasing to Yahweh, as his ancestor David had done. . . . Hez-
ekiah came to the throne when he was twenty-five
years old and reigned for twenty-nine years in
Jerusalem. His mother's name as Abijah, daughter of Zechariah. He did what is pleasing to Yahweh, just as his ancestor David had done.—2
Chronicles 28:1 and 29:1-2*

*"It was I who relieved your shoulder of the
burden . . . you called in your trouble so I rescued
you. . . . Listen, you are my people, let me warn
you. Israel, if you would only listen to me!"—
Psalm 81:6-9*

*"Still happier are those who hear the word
of God and keep it."—Luke 11:28*

*A child of God listens to the words of God;
if you refuse to listen, it is because you are not
God's children.—John 8:47*

If your lips confess that Jesus is Lord and if you believe in your heart that God raised him from the dead, then you will be saved.—Romans 10:10

Chapter 7

Why Doesn't God Heal Everybody Who Asks?

The Junior High children had been discussing prayer with the usual mixture of seriousness and levity. They voiced some good ideas and also some of the conventional, parent-inspired digs at the function of prayer and the reality of answers. God as a far-off magician, as a benevolent dictator, as an unpredictable tyrant had emerged in their talking. At first there was no great depth to what they were saying and I felt frustrated. How does one get across the expanse of God's love and caring to the children of a society which is as sufficient, prideful, superior as ours? Parents whose blasé references to God give Him no more than a name in their lives and the lives of their children make faith hard to develop in an hour a week—some weeks.

But Terry had sat quietly during the whole

lesson, saying nothing but with his deep blue, too-old, too-sad eyes. Finally he spoke and in unison the others hushed to hear him. Terry's father had been killed and his mother had had to be institutionalized from the strain of her loss. He had lived for a large part of his short life with grandparents who had done their best to be what he needed. He adored them. They were all he had, his only security. He was only twelve years old. He needed those grandparents.

"Grandpa had a stroke." His voice was tense and controlled. "He's going to die, the doctor says. Some church people came to pray for him and he's not even better." He stopped. There was silence. Then the discussion began again, on a different level. The children had all seen prayer for healing go unanswered. They had been more aware and caring than I could have guessed.

"My aunt was healed instantly," Dorothy said, thoughtfully. We all knew that her aunt had been a "bad woman" until a dramatic conversion experience.

"God never helps my mother."

"There's no use praying for healing. It doesn't happen."

"I prayed for my cold to get well and it did."

"Colds do anyhow, you know."

Now we were sharing gut-level experiences and now, if I had anything to give the children, I would have my chance. Their remarks were too close to my own emotional level for comfort. My father was in a nursing home for the sixth year, and there was nothing I could do for him but love him. My sister-in-law was dying of slow deterioration. Who was I to answer any of the children's questions?

Still, peace was there, inside my heart. Peace is one of Paul's listed fruits of the Spirit—peace no matter what.

"Holy Spirit, speak your peace to my group of Juniors. They are your beloved children. Here is my voice. You speak . . ."

For the Junior Highs

It is very easy for people to think of God as a magic wand that, if they do the right things, will produce what they want. Lots of people think of prayer that way and of course when they don't get what they have asked God for, they tend to be mad at Him for it. If we think of prayer as just asking God for things, it is easy to become angry at Him. Talking everything over with Him as a friend is a lot different from just begging and begging.

Let's talk over our problem with Him right now. He doesn't always make people well who ask Him to. But sometimes He does. It doesn't seem fair, the way we look at it, because we think that everyone who asks Him for good health would like to have it and should, besides. That is our point of view—but God's is bigger.

Let's imagine that one of you has a sore on his cheek. It isn't very bad, but it does bother you. So you go to the doctor and ask him to give you something to make it well. He examines your cheek and says, "Hmmm." Then he gives

you a lot of other tests—maybe even sends you
to the hospital for some of them. Finally he calls
you into his office and tells you, "The sore on
your cheek is being caused by a blood disorder.
I won't be giving you anything for the cheek, but
I will give you medicine and diets to cure the
blood disease."

That makes sense, doesn't it? You would very
likely be glad that the doctor knew enough to
find out the real trouble and treat it instead of
giving you a bottle of pills or some ointment. But
suppose, instead, that you were *not* pleased. Suppose you were angry at the doctor. After all, he
didn't do a thing about the sore on your cheek.
And he wanted you to do a lot of unpleasant things
like diet and exercise and rest and taking pills,
that you didn't want to do. So you said, crossly,
"That doctor's no good. He didn't even treat what
I went in to see him about!"

God knows all about us, inside and out. He
knows when whatever we have wrong is caused
by bad eating and sleeping habits and when it
is caused by being angry and refusing to forgive.
He knows how we feel inside and what causes
everything we do and think and say. He is a *really*
good doctor.

Supposing the doctor had answered your re-
quest that the little sore on your cheek get well.
He could probably have given some medicine that
would clear it up for a while. But because it was
caused by a deeper kind of sickness, you would
get more sores and some of them would probably
be worse than the one you had in the first place.

God is like that with our prayers. He knows when what we have asked for is the source of the trouble and when it isn't. Sometimes He knows that the only way we can get well is by doing something ourselves—like diet and exercise. Only maybe the "something" we have to do is learn to love and forgive or get rid of negative attitudes or some such thing. When we go to God and ask for healing, we need to ask Him if there is something we should do to help ourselves get well.

So far, the question has been pretty simple. We have compared our unanswered prayers for healing to going to the doctor and hearing that there is something wrong inside us that we didn't know about, which is causing the trouble. But it isn't quite as easy as that. We live in a world with a whole lot of people. Many of them never think to ask God for help. They go on doing things that hurt themselves and others, some of whom don't even know about the fact that someone else is hurting them. Here is an example.

There is a kind of disease that people get that causes their babies to be deformed. Those babies certainly didn't do anything that was wrong. But they are the ones who have the problem. That is because we are all like a family of brothers and sisters. When the little two-year-old boy brings a pile of mud into the house, someone else also gets muddy and someone else also has to clean up. And sometimes the little boy who brings in the mud doesn't even know that mud is not good to have inside the house. Do you see how our troubles are often all connected together so that there is a bigger "disease" than we know about?

Maybe now you are saying to yourself, "What's the use of praying, then? Things are too complicated to make it worth while." That isn't true, though. It is very important for us all to go on asking God for health and help and whatever we need. Just as every crooked stick in a pile of sticks makes the pile more of a mess, every stick that gets straight makes it easier to straighten all the others. If each one of us goes to God and asks Him to help us be healthy and do whatever we need to do to be right with Him and the other people, then it is easier for those around to do it, too. Pretty soon you are the center of a lot of healthy people in the human family. Goodness spreads just as much as badness. Some day the whole world will be healthy and happy because love and goodness are stronger than hate and badness. Even if the thing you first asked for isn't healed, your asking and listening for the answer puts you in the frame of mind to do whatever you can, not just for yourself, but for the whole world.

There's one kind of asking for health that is almost hardest of all. We always want our dear old grandparents and friends to be healthy and happy. We hate to see them hurt and be uncomfortable. We really wish they just wouldn't get old and we hate to think of their dying. So we pray that they'll be well. Usually they aren't or if they do get lots better for a while, they don't stay well and pretty soon they are sick again.

Then we begin to wonder about God's plan and maybe feel angry at Him.

Let's imagine that you have a favorite pair of shoes. They are the best shoes that you've ever had. When a rip comes in one, you take it to the shoe man and get it sewed up. Then the heels wear out and you take it to him again for new heels. After a while, the shoes have so many scuffed places and worn spots that even the best shoe man can't fix them any more. You wear them only for dirty work and you notice that they are uncomfortable. Finally, you begin to think of getting a new pair. All of a sudden, you are excited about having some brand new fresh shoes that fit and are pretty.

Our bodies do wear out. Sometimes they can be fixed up and be in good shape for a time. But eventually they wear clear out. That is part of the good plan God has for all of us. When Jesus was crucified on the cross and then was resurrected and came back to us, He had a new body. It was beautiful and perfect, but it was the same as His old body—enough that the nail holes in His hands and feet still showed. It was the kind of body that could walk through the wall, but it was the kind that could also eat a piece of fish—that people could touch and feel. Jesus told us that we are like Him. We are His brothers and sisters and we will have whatever He has. That means, as Paul told us in his letters, that when the bodies we have wear out, we will get new, perfect, recognizable ones. Just like the shoes, after a certain amount of patching up, there's nothing to do but have new ones. It seems as if God lets the old bodies stay here as long as there is any kind of use for them and then takes them away to make them new.

Old people are often tired of their worn out bodies. They get ready to trade them in on new ones and are not sad about the idea of being perfect in company with Jesus somewhere else. Sometimes it is only those of us who are younger and healthy who are praying for them to get well. That is because we know we will miss them even though we know that they are totally happy with Jesus. God understands that so we don't need to worry if His answer to our prayers is, "It's time for a new body, now, so I'm not going to heal Grandpa again."

There are lots of ways to be sick. Our bodies can be sick and our minds can be sick. Our spirits can be sick, too. If we pray to God for good health, we must ask Him to heal us in all the ways we can be sick. We must ask Him for the rules of good health for body, mind, and spirit, and then do the best we can to follow His suggestions. When everyone in the world has learned to do that, then nobody will ever be sick or sad again. We don't see that happening yet. But if our helping can make it happen sooner, then most of us would rather help than not, wouldn't we?

Scripture

Do not think of yourself as wise, fear Yahweh and turn your back on evil: health-giving, this, to your body, relief to your bones.—Proverbs 3:7-8

Is not this the sort of fast that pleases me—it is the Lord Yahweh who speaks—to break unjust fetters and undo the thongs of the yoke, to let the oppressed go free, and break every yoke, to share your bread with the hungry, and shelter the homeless poor, to clothe the man you see to be naked and not turn from your own kin? Then will your light shine like the dawn and your wound be quickly healed over.—Isaiah 58:6-9

Set your hearts on his kingdom first, and on his righteousness, and all these other things will be given you as well.—Matthew 6:33

Everyone is to recollect himself before eating this bread and drinking this cup; because a person who eats and drinks without recognising the Body is eating and drinking his own condemnation. In fact that is why many of you are weak and ill and some of you have died.—1 Corinthians 11:28-31

My dear people, we are already the children of God, but what we are to be in the future has not yet been revealed; all we know is, that when it is revealed we shall be like him because we shall see him as he really is.—1 John 3:2

Chapter 8

Why Doesn't God Always Punish Bad People?

Mike was in and out of everything that I did in connection with the church from the time he was in kindergarten until he finished high school. We went on choir trips, Sunday school trips, Fellowship trips. Besides that, he was a friend of my children and spent many hours at our house. He was an unusual child: his I.Q. was far above average and he was creativity personified. And, he had that rare quality that allowed him to see and articulate whatever he was feeling. Although he was the age of my own son, almost from his birth, I considered him one of *my* friends.

One day when he was twelve or thirteen he sat on a stool in the kitchen licking the beater and talking to me while the rest of the children entertained themselves outside. He talked a mixture of adult and twelve-year-old, with a little delicate three thrown in, and his sense of humor never failed to enthrall me. But on this day, he seemed worried. We began talking about a man we both knew who seemed to prosper continually at the expense of his fellowman. Mike talked on and on, expressing his doubt in the loving-kindness of a God who would allow such misbehavior. "Fairness" came up over and over again. As I cooked and listened, I began to see that one of the big hang-ups we all have concerning the goodness and love of God stems from our feelings about fairness. From earliest childhood we have been taught to play fair. Rules of games insure fairness, and even our legal systems are designed to make life "fair." We seem to have a built-in awareness, too, of the need for fair play. Or do we? The tiny baby yells for *his* rights. He has to be taught by society, at his own expense, to shape up. And isn't that right? Don't we have a right to expect fairness in what we do? And mustn't we teach our children that?

Those were hard questions to ponder while listening to a fast-talking, beater-licking junior high boy who would soon turn to me and demand to know what I thought of the matter. I took a quick breath and called out, silently, to my Helper, Advocate, Comforter, the Holy Spirit, for some aid, not just for Mike but for me and my own children—for all the people who cry out, "It ain't fair. It just ain't fair!"

For the Junior Highs

Let's think of life as a journey. It starts when we are born and ends—who knows where

—after we have walked through the gate which we call "death." Everyone is on the journey, whether he thinks of it or not. The journey is for a purpose. That purpose is to meet a good Friend. Somehow, inside themselves, people all realize that their lives are a journey and are going somewhere. If they get unhappy, they sometimes wonder where they are going. But the only reason they wonder is because they think they *should* be on the road to something. They feel it in their bones, as the saying goes.

When we are little, our parents help us get started. They lead us on the first part of the journey. Some parents realize that we are going to meet a Friend, and they help their children start in the right direction. They give him road maps and show him how to tell when he is going the right way and when he isn't. They introduce him to other people who know where they are going and how to figure out if they are on the right road.

Other parents have forgotten where the journey is headed, so they don't help their children get going correctly. Still, those children have lots of other people who help them, even where their parents fall down on the job. Nobody in a country like ours, which has books and schools and radio and television, can say that he never heard that he was on a trip to meet a good Friend.

Of course, by now, you know that on the journey of life the good Friend is God, our Father. He is with us and in us, but He is also at the end of our journey through life—just like Grand-

76

pa and Grandma are waiting for us at the end
of a trip to visit them. The people who start their
children toward the right road know that they
have to help us read our road maps so we won't
get lost.

There isn't just one road, though. The world
is full of roads. Some of them are interesting to
explore and follow. Some have beautiful houses
at the end—or even all along the way. Some
have swimming pools and big cars and just about
anything you can think of. They are beautiful
roads. The people on them like them a lot. They
don't remember about the other road that goes
to a Friend's house. They don't know that it has
beautiful things on it, too. In fact, they finally get
to thinking that the road they're on is the only
road there is.

Now let's get back to the thing we started to
talk about in the first place: God's punishing bad
people. If we think of the journey of life, we will
realize that when a person is walking on the
road that leads to God, it isn't very long before
he realizes that his Friend has come to walk with
him. The Friend, who is God, remember, isn't
just waiting somewhere in heaven for us to get
there. Jesus came to earth to show us that God
is with us, loving us just as one friend does another, all the time. When He left after the resurrection (that is called "the ascension"), He told
us that the Holy Spirit would be with us forever
to let us all know that Jesus was walking with
us no matter what happened. So when we begin
on the road toward God, we soon experience the

presence of Jesus through the power of the Holy Spirit. The Holy Spirit is a person, too. So, in a way, we are aware of three Friends instead of one: Father, Son, and Holy Spirit. That makes walking on the path of life quite different from the lonely way we'd feel if we didn't have anyone along. Things are often hard. We get a little lost; we make mistakes; we get hurt. But we're never alone. We always have help. And eventually we get to the house of our Friend and find out what heaven is like, firsthand.

But suppose, instead, that we take a road that leads away from God. Then we have no awareness of the good Friends helping us and leading us and being companions to us. We may do many things that are fun and interesting. We may also do things that are ugly and hurt other people. In fact, a person on a path away from God would be more likely to do mean and ugly things because he would feel lonely inside, and maybe afraid. God does not have to punish a person who is walking alone, without Him. Just being without Him is punishment enough. That is especially true when we think how awful it would be to get to the very end of life and find out that we had not arrived at the home of our Friend. Wouldn't that be a terrible punishment? Do you think God would need to do anything more?

Everything that we are doing on our journey through life is leading us either toward our Friends—Father, Son and Holy Spirit—or it is leading us away from them. So eventually everything that we do gets either "punished" or "rewarded" by getting us either *away* from where we needed to go or *to* where we needed to go (we call it heaven). God doesn't just send down punishment or rewards from heaven willy-nilly.

People are human and not perfect, like God. So, to us, all of life seems to come across as doing things and getting either rewarded or punished. We think it isn't fair if it doesn't turn out that way. We wonder why people who seem to be doing "good things" sometimes have a terribly bad time of it, and we worry because people who are doing "bad things" sometimes seem to be getting alone fine. But God *is* perfect, and He knows that the very most important thing in our lives is being close to Him. Whatever happens to us is to help us with that. It is like on the road we were talking about: sometimes the fastest and best way to get from one point to another is to climb a steep hill. Maybe the hill is rocky and the road is narrow. Maybe we sprain an ankle on the rocks. Still, it is the best road and we take it and try not to complain too much. A person watching us climbing the rough road might say, "That poor man is being punished for nothing. He just hurt himself and he didn't deserve it." All the time the "poor man" might be going up a steep hill, happy that he was in the company of a good Friend and was going to come to that Friend's beautiful home in the mountains pretty soon.

Or suppose a man keeps doing "bad" things and seeming to get away with it. He seems to have lots of money and fame and not ever have to pay for the hurts he causes other people. Only God, who is perfect love, can tell how lonely and hurting the man might be—how he might be trying hard to figure out where the right road is that would lead him to something that he feels missing in his life. And maybe God would let him go on a long time without "punishing" him just because He knows that eventually the man will figure out what is wrong and set himself on the right road. God knows our hearts and can see our whole lives spread out at once. That gives Him a great advantage when He deals with us. And, because He is Love, He always deals with us for the very best. That is something we can seldom see, but we know that He can.

It is much easier to be happy and useful in this life if we know that a good, loving God is in control of the journey. If we feel lost and alone in our travels, then we are terribly unhappy. The best thing each of us can do both for ourselves and for each other is to keep in touch with the Friends who are with us to help us and love us along life's way.

Scripture

Take care your heart is not seduced, that you do not go astray, serving other gods and worshipping them.—Deuteronomy 11:16

He safeguards the steps of his faithful but the wicked vanish in darkness (for it is not by strength that man triumphs).—1 Samuel 2:9

So my heart exults, my very soul rejoices,

my body, too, will rest securely, for you will not abandon my soul to Sheol, nor allow the one you love to see the Pit; you will reveal the path of life to me, give me unbounded joy in your presence, and at your right hand everlasting pleasures.—Psalm 16:9-12

Like a rebel he went the way of his choice; but I have seen the way he went.—Isaiah 57:18

Peter took this up. "What about us?" he asked him. "We have left everything and followed you." Jesus said, "I tell you solemnly, there is no one who has left house, brothers, sisters, father, children, or land for my sake and for the sake of the gospel who will not be repaid a hundred times over, houses, brothers, sisters, mothers, children, and land—not without persecutions—now in this present time and in the world to come, eternal life. Many who are first will be last, and the last first."—Mark 10:28-32

"I will not leave you orphans . . . ."—John 14:18

There must be no passing of premature judgement. Leave that until the Lord comes; he will light up all that is hidden in the dark and reveal the secret intentions of men's hearts.— 1 Corinthians 4:5

We know that we belong to God, but the whole world lies in the power of the Evil One.—1 John 5:19

Chapter 9

How Can I Love My Enemies?

"Christianity isn't really practical in this modern world." (How many times have we all heard that comment?) My Junior High group was angry. They were deep in a hot discussion of a man who had, in their eyes, wronged them all. Someone suggested that Jesus had said that we should love and forgive and pray for our enemies. That did it! How could they possibly love and forgive and pray for a man as terrible as the one they were discussing? Besides, who wanted to? They were enjoying their anger, lending it much hidden fury left over from other times when they had been betrayed and hurt. They used the cop-out that they had heard, not just from non-Christians, but from Christians as well. "Christianity is a good ideal but nobody can do it."

Of course nobody can do it. Christianity is the opposite of every do-it-yourself project there is. Other religions give long lists of things to do. Christianity gives one thing only: believe. With that, all is done—except believe and believe and continue to believe even when it looks as illogical and undesirable as my children were seeing their present problem.

As I listened to the children airing their feelings, I became aware that I, too, was angry. I was angry at all the so-called Christians who had never realized the source of supernatural strength that lies in their believing. And I was angry at churches and educational systems that slide over and miss the real power: the gift that Jesus gave us as He left us to ascend back to the throne of God. After all, Paul and Barnabus and Priscilla and Aquilla and John Mark lived in a world that was no more conducive to forgiving and loving their enemies than ours is. In that respect, the world is no different now than it was 10,000 years ago.

As I acknowledged my own anger and dealt with it, I realized that it was a source of good for me and for the children. It lent me the impetus to speak in a straightforward manner about this modern heresy. If I could reach the children and give them a new focus, they might even carry it home to their parents, thereby giving several people a new approach to life. The only problem was that I wasn't at all sure how to tell them without seeming to criticize their parents and teachers—a thing which I did not want to do.

Children at that middle level have problems enough deciding whether to idolize their parents and copy their every inference or to rebel and live out the exact opposite of everything they have to say. I needed the presence of the Holy Spirit.

"Holy Spirit, I need your power," I said under my breath, and as I did so, the word *power* leaped out at me. Modern children love and respect power. It is almost an idol in many of their homes. "Holy Spirit, pour out your power on this class."

For the Junior Highs

Remember Rip Van Winkle? He went to sleep and slept a long, long time. When he woke up, everyone he had known was old and things were greatly changed. Pretend that you are like Rip Van Winkle and have just awakened from being asleep for 200 years—since our nation first began.

When you wake up, still in your old-fashioned night clothes, it is a hot summer morning. You get up and walk around in your modern 20th-century house. Pretty soon someone comes in and tells you to make the whole room light at once, then to fill it with the music of an orchestra that is from London. Then he tells you to get a handful of little squares of ice and fill a pitcher with water. How do you think you feel? You think, right away, that you have been asked to do a number of quite impossible things.

But then, pretend you get some clothes on and the man who is there with you tells you that now you are to go with him and move the course of a river, fill in a small canyon and then be on the other side of the nation in time to start work there the next afternoon. By that time, you are sure that the whole incident is a bad dream. You probably say that you have been asked to do the impossible and that it is all nonsense—not even sensible enough to consider. You are right, too. For a man who doesn't know anything about the inventions of our time, it would be nonsense all the way from beginning to end.

The way things stand, though, all of those things are easily possible. They are not possible for a person to do with his bare hands. Turning the light on requires that we have electricity in the house. It requires that we have working switches and, of course, know enough to push the switch to "ON." Filling the room with music requires that we have a record player or a radio or a television. Making ice would require a refrigerator or freezer and drawing a pitcher of water would require that we were hooked up to a water supply. None of those things was possible 200 years ago. Nobody had even imagined any of them.

The rest of the tasks the man told you to do would have been even more impossible to accomplish 200 years ago. Nowadays, though, when a contractor takes a contract to change the course of a river and fill in a ravine, he hires men and gives them heavy, powerful equipment to do what needs to be done. And when the men get done, they can fly to the other side of the nation between bedtime and work time the next day on a jet plane.

What we're talking about is power. Nobody could do even the easiest of the jobs we've mentioned without power outside of himself. And that power outside oneself is what makes Christianity not an impossible idealistic religion—one that is nonsense—but a religion that is practical. Think of the man who is going to change the river. If he didn't have a fleet of scrapers and trucks and bulldozers, he wouldn't even try to move the river. That would be impossible. So would getting from San Francisco to New York in one night if we didn't have big jet planes that go faster than sound. Nobody would even consider trying to do those things. They would just say, "That's ridiculous." And it would be, too. And loving our enemies and forgiving people who've hurt us and going an extra mile and turning the other cheek are all just as ridiculous.

The people who say Christianity is an impractical religion are right—if they don't know about the power that God has given us to do those things. He is just like the contractor who hires a man to work for him. The contractor would never tell someone to do a job that the man couldn't do unless he gave the man the equipment to do it. Neither did Jesus. He gave us the tools to do everything He told us we should do.

Many people don't know about the power that Jesus gave us to do the impossible things that He talked to us about. That's why they call Him a dreamer and an idealist and why they often don't come to Him and let Him help them. We need to help everyone find out about the power

that makes Christianity different from other religions. That power is the Holy Spirit. He is like
a piece of big machinery in one way. He can
do what people can't do by themselves. And He
is like electricity in another way. He can take
ordinary wire and ordinary voices and ordinary
glass bulbs and make lights and music and va-
cuum and ice and hundreds of things that we
can't do without. And He is like jet planes in
another way because He can move us faster and
farther than we could ever go on our own. He
moves us in many different ways. Sometimes He
surprises us with getting us changed from one
place to another physically, like a ride when we
don't expect it or all the schedules fitting together
when we expected to wait. And sometimes He
moves us from being very angry and upset to
being happy and forgiving.

The Holy Spirit is the one who makes it possible for us to do impossible things. Nobody in all
the world could ever love his enemies without
help. Even in the Old Testament, the people didn't
understand that they could ever love their enemies. And people who don't know about the Holy
Spirit still don't understand how it can be done.
But when the power, which comes from the Spirit,
arrives in our lives, then we find ourselves loving
and forgiving and doing all sorts of creative things
that we didn't know how to do before. We find
out that you can really love even without having
any sentimental or romantic feelings about someone. We find out that you can forgive and forget
even the worst kinds of bad things people have

done. And, besides that, you can know that if you needed to, you could help and comfort your enemies as if they were your friends. All of those things are as impossible as changing the course of the river with your bare hands—unless you have some sort of power to do them that is bigger and stronger than yourself.

When Jesus left, He told His disciples that after He had gone they would receive power from on high. He also told them that their comforter or Advocate or Helper would come. The titles are different in different translations of His language, but they all mean the same thing: Someone to help us do what we can't do on our own. And that is exactly how the power of the Holy Spirit works. When we can't forgive or love, He helps us. He makes it possible; in fact, through us, for things to happen, like light in the darkness and music when there's no orchestra, and love when there has been only hatred. The Holy Spirit is the power like electricity and machinery and water power, but He is more than all of these, because He is also a person. He is a friend. A big bulldozer isn't understanding and gentle. It is only machinery. But the Holy Spirit is powerful and kind and loving as well. The next time someone says Christianity is impractical and Jesus told us to do things that are impossible in our modern world, feel sorry for that person because he hasn't met the power that accomplishes the impossible. Maybe you'll even get a chance to tell him about that power.

Scripture

As he approached Lehi, and the Philistines came running toward him with triumphant shouts, the spirit of Yahweh seized on Samson; the ropes on his arms became like burnt strands of flax and the bonds melted off his hands. Catching sight of the fresh jawbone of a donkey, he reached out and snatched it up; then with it he struck down a thousand men.—*Judges 15:14-16*

"We ourselves do not know what to do; we look to you (God)."—2 Chronicles 20:12

A curse on the man who puts his trust in man, who relies on things of flesh, whose heart turns from Yahweh. . . . A blessing on the man who puts his trust in Yahweh, with Yahweh for his hope.—*Jeremiah 17:5 and 7*

"And now I am sending down to you what the Father has promised. Stay in the city then, until you are clothed with the power from on high."—Luke 24:49

What the Spirit brings is very different: love, joy, peace, patience, kindness, goodness, trustfulness, gentleness, and self-control.—*Galatians 5:22*

God's gift was not a spirit of timidity, but the Spirit of power, and love, and self-control.—2 Timothy 1:7

Chapter 10

Why Do We Have to Have All the Rituals and Stuff?

The Junior Highs had been asked to wash and fill the communion cups, and they were happily doing the chore, making it as noisy and dangerous as possible. I was mentally noting that we had only seventeen spares and wishing the job were over when I noticed an ever-so-slight change in the focus.

"Communion's the best, but I think they're all a bore," someone was saying. I listened more carefully.

"Yeah. Half the time in church, we've gotta go over things written down in a book. We've gotta read just words and words."

"I don't think communion's the best. It just takes forever for all those people."

I noted several heads nodding and smiles of

agreement on a number of faces. Sally, though, seemed near tears. I touched her shoulder in sympathy.

"You like communion, don't you, Sally?" I whispered. Her face glowed; her eyes were grateful. The others went on with their comments and I stood lost in thought. These children knew about communion. They knew about many of the church rituals and sacraments. They had been in classes and had correctly answered the questions concerning the doctrines in which they were participating. And I had been in their place myself, I had to admit: where I daydreamed through responsive readings and counted the clicks of the clock until all the people had come up and received communion.

Junior High is a teetery time, at best. Many children drop out of all church activities soon after that age. But some don't. If "something clicks," as my daughter said once, then they stay and are ripe for a deep love commitment to Jesus. And Sally? Why did she have such a different response? Could I find a clue to help my dozen children come to a new understanding—or at least patience with this phase of our church activity?

Not by myself, I couldn't. What had changed my own feelings toward the sacraments and the rituals? I didn't know. For years they were negative and then, one day, as if I had come back after an absense, they turned positive. Holy Spirit, you will have to fit the pieces of this puzzle together for me.

For the Junior Highs

Let's begin by pretending that you have gone on a perfectly wonderful trip. You have taken a ship across the ocean. You have stood on the deck with a special someone with whom you have fallen in love. You have had loads of fun with all sorts of interesting people and then, finally, you have gone to one after another of the most exciting places imaginable. The trip has taken a long time—months, maybe. So, to make sure that you don't forget any of the great experiences you have had and the things you've learned and the people you've met, you have been careful to keep a complete scrapbook. You have written down the names of people and places; you have pasted ticket stubs and programs into your scrapbook. You have maps and photographs of all the interesting places and all kinds of information. You have even included pieces of cloth and dried flowers that you have been able to get so that you'd have a memory of even the feel and smell of the things you saw.

That scrapbook is a work of art. So, of course, you are proud of it. You take it home and call your family together to look at it. You think that if they look at all of the pictures and samples that you have in the scrapbook, it will be almost as good as going to the places and seeing the things you have seen.

At first the members of your family do seem thrilled with the scrapbook. They listen to you tell about your experiences and appear to be really interested. But pretty soon you notice that they are getting a bit bored. You try hard to make the pictures come alive for them. It doesn't do any good. After a while they begin to drift away and finally they let you know for sure that the whole idea doesn't interest them at all. It is disappointing; but there just isn't anything you can do to make them care for your experiences.

Well, suppose some more. Suppose that a boy who was on most of the trip with you comes to visit. You get out your scrapbook and sit down with him on the sofa. The two of you get your heads together over the pictures and programs and names and before long you realize that you've seldom had so much fun in your life. The evening goes so fast that you can't believe it is over. You invite the boy to come again the next evening and when he comes, you start right in at the beginning of the scrapbook and look all the way through again. It seems almost as much fun as the first time. You recall things you had almost forgotten and you remind him of things he didn't remember. You spend a second happy evening over your scrapbook.

Every once in awhile, even months after the trip is over, you and your friend get out the book and look at it again. It seems as if you can relive the trip that way—even get some new ideas and insights about what happened. You remember people, too, and maybe get busy and write some of them letters to keep in touch.

Still, your family is bored when you try to

show your things to them. You can't really get them to have the feelings you did on the trip, no matter how carefully you show and explain the scrapbook to them. That is true until your little brother gets old enough to be on a trip himself. Then everything changes in a hurry. As soon as he comes back, he is interested in your scrapbook. He wants to see and hear about everything in it that he saw and did on *his* trip. You go over the book and compare experiences. You relive some of the events you enjoyed and tell him things he missed. Then he tells you some of the sights you missed. You spend a lot of happy times together sharing your experiences. The objects and pictures in your scrapbook take on new meaning—especially when your other friend comes over and the three of you talk about what happened to each of you on the trip.

The sacraments in our churches are a lot like the scrapbook from your trip. They are ceremonies that we do to relive experiences that have meant a lot to us. Every time we do one of them, it is the same sort of feeling that we have when we look at a scrapbook full of souvenirs. When we do the thing over and over, we get the same thrill as we did the first time we did it. We smell the flowers and hear the music, for example, when we look at a program for a very special party. We feel our special friend near us, or taste the special cake and punch. It is a way to remember.

And more than a nice way to remember, it

is also a way to find out all the good things that happened—sometimes so fast that we might have missed some if we didn't go over them and think about them.

Let's consider communion, for example. The original disciples who were with Jesus at the Last Supper ate and drank their communion meal again and again in memory of Jesus. They knew that there were a lot of hidden meanings and ideas they might have missed the first time they had communion at the Last Supper, so every time they took communion, they thought and talked about everything it meant to them. They could feel the presence of Jesus in their midst just as if He had never left them to go back to God. And of course, that is the way He had told them it would be. He had told them that He was sending the Holy Spirit to them to help them go on seeing and hearing their beloved Jesus just as if He were still eating with them in the flesh. They loved communion very much. They made it a thing that they passed on to other people who were born after Jesus had gone back to heaven. Those people never saw Him until the Holy Spirit let them experience His presence. They didn't see Him like the first disciples did—in the flesh. They had to depend on the Holy Spirit to help them get acquainted with Jesus.

You remember that we talked about how bored your family was with the scrapbook? They were especially bored after they had seen it once. The reason they were bored was that the scrapbook was just a collection of programs and names and pictures to them. When your friend came over, you and he enjoyed the scrapbook because it reminded you of the ways you had felt when you were on your trip and had nearly forgotten. You could discuss those feelings and ideas again, which was fun. Looking at the scrapbook didn't make your family have those feelings and ideas, so they found it boring. The experiences had to come first to make the souvenirs exciting.

That is what happens, sometimes, at rituals like communion. The people who have never felt the presence of Jesus eating and talking and working with them are much more likely to be bored at the ritual of communion than the people who have had the experience of His love in their lives. We can't usually get them to have that experience of His love in their lives. We can't usually get them to have the experience of Jesus by making them take communion with us, no matter how much we want to. The Holy Spirit can, but we can't. It is like showing the scrapbook to the little brother. Before he had taken the trip himself, he was bored with the book. But after he had been in all those places, then he liked to share the book, the talk, and the recounting of all those experiences.

Other church rituals are the same way. It is sort of human nature to want to have a memorial of a really great or exciting time. We take home a souvenir from a beautiful picnic or a fun party, a new place, a new friend. Taking home a souvenir seems to make the experience last longer and help us not to forget whatever was especially nice

or important about it. The same thing is true
in our churches. Maybe a special Friend, Jesus,
did something with a man long ago and the man
wrote a little ceremony to remember it by. It
made another man think of a similar experience
he had had, so that man wrote the ceremony into
our prayer book. Every time another person had
a similar experience, he came and enjoyed the
ceremony because it reminded him of what had
happened to him. It goes without saying that if
you were reading that ceremony and you had
never had any experience the least bit like that,
you might be bored.

Nobody can make another person enjoy the
scrapbook unless that other person has some interest of his own in it. The same thing is true
of our church rituals. We go at things backwards
if we try to make people have the experiences
the rituals are about by just going over and over
the rituals. What we need to do is help them find
out who their wonderful Friend, Jesus, really is
and then they will love reading a scrapbook
about Him. They will love all the rituals because
they will be reliving great times the rituals make
them think of—great times with that very, *very*
best Friend.

There's one more thing, too, about rituals. If
you have made an important promise to someone,
every time you read the words of the promise,
you will, inside yourself, make it again as you
read. If we have promised Jesus that we will
love and follow Him, then every time we read
the words that pledge to love and follow Him over,

we promise again. That feels good. It helps us keep on the right track and not forget that He is the most important person in our lives. If we had never made that promise in the first place, just reading those words over and over again would really get a bit tiresome. It's better to find the person first and then make our promises directly to Him. After that the rituals are happy reminders of a good experience.

Scripture

But until today Yahweh has given you no heart to understand, no eyes to see, no ears to hear.— Deuteronomy 29:4

"Is the pleasure of Yahweh in holocausts and sacrifices or in obedience to the voice of Yahweh?"—1 Samuel 15:22

I know that you are all-powerful: what you conceive, you can perform. I am the man who obscured your designs with my empty-headed words. I have been holding forth on matters I cannot understand, on marvels beyond me and my knowledge. . . . I knew you then only by hearsay; but now, having seen you with my own eyes, I retract all I have said, and in dust and ashes I repent.—Job 42:2-5

Then he took some bread, and when he had given thanks, broke it and gave it to them, saying, "This is my body which will be given for you; do this as a memorial of me." He did the same with the cup after supper, and said, "This cup is the new covenant in my blood which will be poured out for you. . . ."—Luke 22:19-21

Until the Lord comes, therefore, every time you eat this bread and drink this cup, you are proclaiming his death, and so everyone who eats the bread or drinks the cup of the Lord unworthily will be behaving unworthily towards the body and blood of the Lord.—1 Corinthians 11:27

Chapter 11

Why Was God So Mean to Jesus?

At first it bothered me that the middle-sized children seem to be angry so often about matters of religion. Why in the world, I wondered, do they get so upset whenever they let down their defenses and speak their real feelings? And it seemed to me that they were always calling on me to justify God's action. Finally I understood. They are angry and defensive because they want so very much for it all to "turn out right." They hope with every cell of their bodies that there is a good, loving God who has everything under His control. In fact it is so important to them that they will often refuse to examine anything that hints of disillusion, shrugging it off, instead, as foolishness.

I guess that we were constructed with that characteristic by God himself. Great thinkers have called it a "God-shaped hole" in us—filled by nothing else but Him. At any rate, after I realized the fact that anger is a sign of true caring, I found it easier to deal with. The children did not want to have that anger. They wanted me to, in fact, stand up for God—and win my case. This I could never do by myself. Trying to justify and defend the Bible and the actions of God is self-defeating. More than that, it is unnecessary. He can defend himself. I need only be His witness and speak what I know, have heard and seen. He will then do the rest. And even if my own sense of fairness and my own ideas about how things should be are totally disappointed, it is still possible for me to have the deep knowledge that I just don't understand some far greater plan. This feeling often saved the day for me in dealing with Junior High children. Those little/big people are emerging. They are sorting what are their parents' and what are their teachers' and finding, finally, some ideas of their own. They are caught up in what is "right and wrong," "fair and un- fair," "logical and illogical." They truly believe that many ideas are their own discoveries, when they came, in fact, directly from some hurt or disturbed adult. So even when they required me to explain God's actions, it was up to me not to let them put me on the defensive. He doesn't stand or fall on the basis of what *anyone* can prove about Him. Paul said, "Will God be un- faithful just because I am unfaithful? Of course not!" What I had to do with the children was to let God do His own speaking. I could offer Him my mouth, my voice, my vocabulary. But

He had to furnish the insights.

I had figured all that out one Sunday—just in time for a very tense moment among my children. Mary was hotly parroting her mother (whom I had heard make the same statement) and her near-tears voice was begging me to set her at rest.

"I don't love God. I hate Him. He was so mean to Jesus. Why would a God who is supposed to be loving be so mean to His Son?" The other young people added their comments, apparently glad that someone had finally said what was on their minds. I took a deep breath.

"This one's for you, Lord," I said silently to Him, not having the least idea what my—or any—answer could be to Mary and the others.

"Take over, please . . ."

For the Junior Highs

Have you ever noticed that most people love fairy stories? They always have. Fairy stories are in every country and in every language. Some of them are so old that nobody has any idea when they began. One of the reasons that people like fairy stories is that they turn out right. The wicked witch gets killed and the prince and princess marry and are happy together. But they don't turn out right too easily. They have a lot of suspense. There's always a time in the middle of fairy stories when it looks as if goodness couldn't possibly win out. But it always does because some good fairy or the kind king or something that is bigger and better than the bad comes along to turn the tide.

Have you ever noticed, too, that there is a pattern about most of the fairy stories and myths? In a great many of them there is an old king who has a talented and handsome son. The son is in love with a beautiful princess or he meets her and falls in love with her after the story begins. But there is a dragon or a wicked witch or some other bad thing that is stopping the proper working of the kingdom and the proper coming together of the prince and the princess who are in love. The king sends his son, who is, of course, the best and handsomest and most talented person in the kingdom, to kill the witch or steal the magic or get rid of the dragon or whatever is the trouble in their lives. The prince nearly always has a hard time. He nearly gets killed or he is kidnapped or the job is so hard that only the good magic of some kind fairy helps him do it. The worst kinds of things always happen to him and if he were just an ordinary person instead of the king's son, he could never get through. Sometimes, in the stories, the prince is even killed and only when the love of a princess comes along does he recover.

Have you ever wondered why the person who saved the kingdom, in those fairy stories, had to be the prince: the very finest, smartest, kindest person in the kingdom? There is a reason. It's the same reason that when you want to buy something very special and valuable, you know that you will have to pay a lot of money for it. Even if something at the dime store looks pretty, even looks like the valuable article, you know that if it only costs ten cents, it isn't very good quality. In order to get something that is made of fine materials and done carefully and well, a person has to pay for it. If the king sent a stupid man to do the job of killing the dragon, then the dragon might outwit him and kill him, instead. If he sent a man who was clumsy and couldn't run very fast, the dragon might catch him and bite him. The man that he sent would have to be a better man than whatever bad thing he had set out to conquer. In the old days in most kingdoms it was only the kings' sons who were well fed and well educated, so if they were smart and healthy at all, they were usually the best prepared in the kingdom to do challenging things.

Now let's put all these things together to see if they give us a hint about why God seemed to be so mean to His Son, Jesus. The old fairy stories were made up, of course. But they were based on some truths that have been true as long as mankind has existed. One of the truths is that in order to conquer anything, one has to be stronger than it is. That seems pretty obvious, doesn't it? But think about all the evil in the world rolled into one big glob. Instead of killing one dragon or one wicked witch, think about the prince having to defeat that great glob of wickedness all at once. He would have to be some super person. No ordinary man could even look at that kind of job. But God's only Son was not an ordinary man. He was, and still is, God as well as man. He could do anything God could do. He could have just done away with all wickedness at once if He'd wanted to.

Why do you suppose He didn't? Wouldn't it have been better to be done with all wickedness at once, forever and forever? The problem was that because God had given mankind free choice to know about bad and choose bad if they wanted to, every single man in the world, since Adam, had chosen some bad—a lot, in fact. Nobody ever lives all love and nothing else. But that is what God would like for us to do. God created us in love and He loves us no matter how bad we are. *However,* He doesn't love the badness itself. If He destroyed all the badness in the world at once, there wouldn't be much left of His people. We'd mostly be destroyed, too. So He didn't just send down a bolt of lightning and destroy all evil. He didn't because He loves us. We are like the princess in the fairy story. He loves us but He has to rescue us from evil before we can be married and live happily ever after. In between the princess and the prince is a large area that is controlled by wickedness. The prince has to be stronger and wiser than the wickedness to get through it and save the princess.

Remember that we talked about things that are valuable costing a lot? The prince loves the princess but he knows that he will have to pay a high price to get her for his wife. He will have to be brave enough to give his life if he has to in order to win her away from her prison or the dragon or the wicked witch. He will have to fight and bleed and give up everything to defeat evil and save the princess. He knows she is worth saving, so he is willing to do it. The king knows that it is worth doing, so, no matter how much he loves his son, he tells him to go ahead and fight the dragon. The king knows that he would be very sad if his son were killed. However, he also knows that some things are valuable enough to run the risk.

The people who made up old fairy stories knew about some truths, you see, and what Jesus did was act out the fairy stories in person—in the person of God—and make them real. It was like dreaming about spring before it comes or play-acting marriage before you were old enough to have a husband or wife. Jesus was the finest and best and most valuable man who ever lived because He was God as well as man. So He was the King's Son. (God himself was the King.) The King's Son had to go right into the dragon's den to challenge and beat the dragon. Jesus had to go right up to the cross and have the worst things that were possible to happen to anybody happen to Him in order to show evil that goodness is stronger. He had to allow himself to experience the worst there is in order to pay the price to redeem the princess. God had showed the Israelites a long time before that we can make a blood sacrifice to find forgiveness if we repent and are sorry. Jesus made a blood sacrifice with His own blood, just as the prince, in the fairy stories, risked everything to kill the witch or the dragon.

God didn't make Jesus die on the cross. Jesus did it of His own free will. Just like the prince in our fairy stories, Jesus loved the princess (all of the people) enough to risk everything to win her away from the ugly dragon. He knew that until He challenged evil and won the battle, He would never have showed that He really was the Son of the King. The King was sad that His Son had to do such a hard thing, but can you imagine His saying that the Prince mustn't do it? Of course not.

Then how did Jesus defeat evil? He did it by experiencing death—just as bad a death as there was—and then coming back to life again. He showed the dragon (or Satan, or the witch, all of which are names we have for evil) that He could conquer evil once and for all. He didn't stop with just coming back to life again either. He did more than that. He left some of the power which He used to conquer death for those of us who love Him to have too. He sent the Holy Spirit to help us remember that evil is really destroyed. Sure, we all know that there is lots of evil around us, but it is a defeated dragon. If we just remember to call out the name of Jesus, the Prince, and remind the evil that He has defeated it, then it will turn and run. What Jesus did was to make all the evil in the world so afraid of Him that nobody who has Him for a Friend ever needs to be afraid again.

God, the King, is also a very loving Father. He loves His Son and He loves all of His people. He was proud to have such a fine Son who could defeat the bad witch and the dragon and win the Kingdom for Him. He knew that His Son was strong enough to win over evil and when He let Him go into the battle, He knew that the story would turn out right finally. We know that it did, too, even when things seem to be going wrong. Paul said, "All things work for good for them that love the Lord and follow in His ways." He said that because he could see that life is like the fairy story: the Prince has defeated the dragon and won the princess. Lots of people just don't know that He has. If they knew that the "story" has a happy ending, they would be able to live victoriously "in the name of Jesus."

Scripture

Yahweh judges the ends of the earth, he endows his king with power, he exalts the horn of his Anointed.—1 Samuel 2:10

Yahweh says this to you, "Do not be afraid, do not be daunted by this vast horde; this battle is not yours but God's."—2 Chronicles 20:15

Here is my servant whom I uphold, my chosen one in whom my soul delights. I have endowed him with my spirit that he may bring true justice to the nations. He does not cry out or shout aloud, or make his voice heard in the streets. He does not break the crushed reed, nor quench the wavering flame. Faithfully he brings true justice; he will neither waver, nor be crushed until true justice is established on earth, for the islands are awaiting his law.—Isaiah 42:1-4

Yes, God loved the world so much that he gave his only Son, so that everyone who believes in him may not be lost but may have eternal life.—*John 3:16*

Give in to God, then; resist the devil and he will run away from you.—*James 4:8*

Chapter 12

What Good Does It Do to Pray for Other People?

Jan came to our group from some other church; and it didn't take my children or me five minutes to see that she was "different." Our Community church is liberally full of differences. We go all the way from liberal to fundamental in our Sunday school classes, mostly depending upon the stance of the teacher. The church itself changes with the minister and the board. But Jan was more different than anybody else we had had in the class. For one thing, she was serene. She was so at peace inside herself that the other children, full of doubts and questions, reacted against her. They called her smug and snooty and tried their best to upset her calm. They never did. And of course that infuriated them. I often worried that Jan was only putting on an act—that some day the testing of the other children would

finally tear down her defense and leave her dev-
astated. It never happened. All year long they dug
away at her assurance and when she finally left
to go back where she came from, they had yet to
upset her. I'm sure she was lonely and I'm sure
she would have liked to have them relate to her
as a member of their group. But she seemed able
to manage her feelings and come out with true
grace and compassion. I almost envied her whatever it was she had. We all needed it. And I think
perhaps the other children envied her, too.

The day we came the nearest to finding out
the source of Jan's inner strength, I think we
would have broken through to a new place of hap-
piness for ourselves if I had known *before* class
what I realized during class. I guess the timing
wasn't right. Maybe the children weren't ready
yet. Or maybe I wasn't myself. Teachers grow
with the class. If I had known beforehand some
of what I found out as I taught those Junior High
young people—well, I probably wouldn't have
taught them.

One of the girls had started telling about a
problem the members of her family were en-
meshed in. She would have liked to stop relating
it, but the class was interested. They kept asking
questions. And in a way it was good for her to
unload her grief. Finally she got the whole story
out and the class sat with nothing to say. Embar-
rassment overcame them all. They shifted and
tried to start some foolishness. It fell flat. Then,
into the quiet, Jan spoke: "I'll get my family
to pray for your family."

Everyone turned to her, almost in anger. "Who pray?" "Why pray?" "What good does it do to pray for someone else?" The questions flew.

Jan answered quietly: "We all pray together: Dad and Mom and my brother and my sisters."

The class looked at her in disbelief: "When?"

"Any time. At breakfast and lunch and in the evening. And if there's a problem." A veritable barrage of doubt hit Jan in the face. At the bottom was their solid affirmation that *that* kind of prayer just couldn't work.

"Yes it does. It works all the time." Jan's voice was even. "I don't know how. I just know it does."

The children shrugged and looked at me to explain. I sensed that underneath their pretended sophistication was the deep wish that I would convince them that prayer "like that" was effective. I knew that it was, but I had no idea how to tell them so. Concrete reality was all they would listen to, and even that would be contaminated by the ever-present concept of "coincidence." But it was a moment of divine importance. I felt it in every part of me. If the Spirit would speak, I would gladly offer my voice for Him to use. If He wouldn't, there was nothing I could do. I prayed my favorite prayer: "Help!"

For the Junior Highs

Suppose you have found a puppy, adopted him, and become very fond of him. He has responded to your love. You are teaching him tricks and the two of you make a happy pair. Then suppose he gets sick. You think he is sick because he has worms. So you take him to the vet, who is also a friend of yours. You tell the vet, "I brought my puppy to you because I know you know a lot about dogs and their diseases. I think he has worms and I think you should give him worm medicine. But I might be wrong. That is the way it looks to me, but if you know something else about him, go ahead and do whatever he needs."

The vet begins to examine the dog. But the poor little fellow is very much afraid of the vet. He trembles all over. The vet looks him over carefully and then decides he needs some pills. He knows that the puppy trusts you, so he gets you to give the puppy the pills. He says, "I'll let you be my hands for me because the little dog knows you and trusts you. You were right about the worms. He does need worm medicine. He also needs some other things, which I will give you to give him."

Now praying for someone you love is a lot like you and the vet and the puppy. You love the puppy very much. He responds to that love and loves you back. Because you love him you know when he is hurting and you go to someone you are sure knows a lot and ask for help. You tell what you think is the trouble and suggest what you think is a good cure. Then you tell the Person that you concede His greater wisdom and, in spite of what you might think of the trouble, you will help to do whatever He suggests. The puppy responds to the fact that you love him, that you have teamed up with Someone who knows more than you do, and that that Someone has given him treatment.

The puppy may not know the vet, so he will not respond to what the vet needs to do. But he knows you. In a way you are the only hands God has to love some people with when they don't know Him or His love. Your prayer is love and no matter what the vet (God) does, the puppy (whoever you pray for) will feel the power of being loved. And whenever a person goes to God with a problem, God does do something. We may not understand what He does, but if we are aware of what is happening at all, we will notice things being done. We have suggested a solution, which may or may not be right. The very fact that we have teamed up with Love in Person will help us to see what kind of medicine the doctor is giving our puppy.

The next part of the process of praying for other people involves praying for them from a distance. If God really does know everything and we don't know at all what someone on the other side of the country needs, then it seems silly to pray for him. It would make more sense to pray for the person we're with, because he feels our love and responds to our teaming up with God the healer to ask for help for him. That *seems* to be true because it makes sense to us. Things are different with God. God is love and love is power—the strongest power that exists. If you pretend that you are an electric cord with a plug on the end and plug yourself into that power by deliberately putting yourself as open to God as you can, then you can be just like a big broadcasting station. You can beam love and caring all over the country. Distance doesn't make much difference to the big power which is love. You can be a station that broadcasts the fact that you are teaming up with God to turn a large stream of love in the direction of a person even if he is in India or Africa.

Now supposing that you and your whole family take hold of hands and plug into the power at the same time, like a giant cable all twisted together. You can beam a bigger stream of love if you all send your power in the same direction just like some radio stations have 50,000 watts while others just have 20,000. The more people who pray for the same thing together, the more love is sent to the same place. It puts the person who is being prayed for into a regular cloudburst of love. You are the channel that aim's God's love. The person who is being prayed for feels things happening. Sometimes he doesn't know what's happening or that anybody is praying for him. But he knows that things are going on in his life. Loving him by praying for him makes him long for God—even if he doesn't know what he is feeling.

Have you ever just had a feeling inside that made you uncomfortable without knowing what it was? Sometimes after a while you discovered you were hungry or thirsty or had a rock in your shoe. Longing for God is like that. People hunt around and do things and try things until finally someone comes along and tells them that they need to meet Jesus. When they do that, then they feel like you do when you're hungry and finally get your lunch. Praying for people a great way off or right beside you will eventually make them long for Jesus. Even if you don't know how else to pray, you can always beam love toward someone in another place. When you ask God to touch their lives, He will cover people with His love. God wants His love to be the most important thing in everyone's life. So when you team up with Him for that, all kinds of things begin to happen.

You may be wondering why, if God knows everything, it makes any difference whether we pray for anybody at all or not. There is an answer to that. God never did make us to be puppets. God wants us to love because we choose to instead of because He pulls strings and makes us. He has given us the choice of being teamed up with His power because we choose to plug in, or of ignoring it altogether. He usually doesn't push anybody around and make him change unless the person wants to. But He really wants everybody to love Him because God *is* love. He has given us free choice. If we use our free choice to turn to Him and ask some good thing for another person, God must be so happy (because we are not only turning to Him ourselves but are also hoping to get someone else to turn) that He just piles on the extra love. And you know how great it is when you feel all that love. We never do know what special good things will happen when we pray for other people. We can't even guess. All we know is that everyone involved, ourselves included, has good tingles inside at having been part of the 50,000-watt power station.

Scripture

. . . then if my people who bear my name humble themselves, and pray and seek my presence and turn from their wicked ways, I myself will hear from heaven and forgive their sins and restore their land. Now and for the future my eyes are open and my ears attentive to the prayer that is offered in this place.—2 Chronicles 7:14-15

For Yahweh has heard the sound of my weeping; Yahweh has heard my petition, Yahweh will accept my prayer.—Psalm 6:9

"Lord, teach us to pray, just as John taught his disciples."—Luke 11:1

Pray all the time, asking for what you need, praying in the Spirit on every possible occasion.—Ephesians 6:18

Be happy at all times; pray constantly; and for all things give thanks to God, because that is what God expects you to do in Christ Jesus.—1 Thessalonians 5:16-17

The prayer of faith will save the sick man and the Lord will raise him up again; and if he has committed any sins, he will be forgiven. So confess your sins to one another, and pray for one another, and this will cure you; the heartfelt prayer of a good man works very powerfully.—James 5:15-18

Chapter 13

Why Are There So Many Rules?

It was easy to be sympathetic with the Junior High young people when they started discussing their confusion about rules. It was plain to see that some of them were burdened with unreasonably restrictive rules; while others had so few guidelines that they lived in a constant state of insecurity. And I had four children of my own. My personal confrontation with the problem of what to insist on was ever-present.

"Even the Bible's nothing but a bunch of rules," Billy said vehemently. They knew better than that. We had often discussed the wealth of material in the Bible. Still, I knew how the children were feeling. Everything comes across to match a prejudice, even in the Bible.

One of the problems we all have is that suggestions and statements seem like pronouncements. If I am insecure and someone gives me his opinion, I feel pushed around and threatened.

Children in those middle years, with their burden to find out who they are, have a particularly difficult time accepting any kind of suggestion. Besides, they want and need certain guidelines and a reasonable amount of positive authority. They are caught between being children and being adults with no firm ground on either side. It takes a tremendous amount of patience and tact to relate to them. Like goldfish they dart away from anything threatening, from confrontation unless they have initiated it. Yet from the bottom of their hearts they want to be guided and trusted and loved, helped, respected, treated as worthwhile individuals—while not always acting as if they deserve any of it. If I had to do my life over again, the last part that I would choose to relive would be Junior High. And I was there long before anyone thought of that as being a "difficult age." To our parents, we were still children playing on the sidewalk. The girls in my class now are young women, knowledgeable young adults wearing nylon hose and sometimes more up on the "way things are" than I am. And still they remain children needing my help and guidance and comfort.

"Lord, I am in over my head. If I have anything to say to the children about 'rules,' it is going to have to come straight from you!"

For the Young People

Let's think for a little while about people growing up from babies to adults. When babies are first new, they don't have much to say about what

happens to them. They can cry, but they are de-
pendent on someone else for everything. If a baby
has good, loving parents, they will try to give
him what he needs when he cries. But if he doesn't,
then he's just out of luck. Someone else makes
all the baby's rules for him: when to eat and
what to eat and what to wear. Most parents do
the best they can to help their babies grow proper-
ly.

Pretty soon every baby grows into a little
toddler. He can do some things for himself and
decide some things for himself. He has learned
some ways of making the rules. You've seen a
little tot in a playpen throw his toy out of the
pen and then try to get someone to get it for
him. But his parents still have to put him in a
playpen or if he is on the floor, they put a fence
across the stairway and turn all the cooking pan
handles toward the back of the stove. Why do
you suppose they do all those things? It is because the baby could very easily kill himself if
they didn't. They make a lot of "no-no" rules
and enforce them because the baby doesn't know
enough yet to be allowed to decide what he can
do. As he gets older, he can see the reason why
he shouldn't do some things and then the fences
and barriers don't have to be there any more.
A three-year-old child has learned to go up and
down stairs and to keep away from the "hot"
and to do a lot of thinking for himself.

Still, there are many rules that parents still
have to make for a three-year-old. He absolutely
mustn't turn on the ignition and play with the

starter in the car. And he mustn't cross a busy street. He mustn't play with the bottles in the medicine cabinet. He knows some things but he still doesn't know enough to get along by himself. Later, as he gets bigger, he can cross the street and buy groceries at the store. But he still can't start up the car. He still can't go alone in a boat or travel by himself. He can't decide a lot of things, yet, and he still has to follow someone else's rules.

The older people get, the more they are supposed to learn to think for themselves. They are supposed to learn how the rules were made and why and then act on the reason for each rule instead of just following it. For example, if a little boy had always lived in a home where people loved and cared for each other and other people, he would probably understand that he mustn't cross the street because it was dangerous. But if he saw his friend on the other side of the street choking on his jacket string, he would probably break the rule and go help him. He would do that because he would be following a bigger rule: that we care for other people and help them when they are in trouble.

We have lots of rules that we have to follow all the time. Some, like "Keep off the grass," are rules that are to make life more pleasant for everyone. Others, like "Don't run at the swimming pool," are for the general safety. If you have an allergy and the doctor makes a rule that you are not to eat whatever you are allergic to, that rule is for your comfort. The rule that

you are not to kill other people is something altogether different. If you break that one, it is
much more serious than breaking a "Keep off
the grass" kind of rule.

When Jesus came, He gave us one big rule
that is more important than every other rule in
the world. His rule is that everything is to be
done in love. A tiny baby doesn't know much about
love. He can't follow that rule. So he has to follow
rules that other people have made for him. But
those rules are made out of love for him. His
parents love him so they make rules that keep
him safe and healthy. After he gets bigger he
begins to find out about love and then he can
start to be loving. It takes a long, long time to
learn all about love. Probably if we lived a hundred and fifty years we wouldn't know all there
is to know. But we would know some things about
it. And each thing we learned would help us decide how to behave.

Rules in the Bible are just like rules our parents make. They are to help us live without dam-
aging ourselves or other people. Look at every
rule you can think of. They were basically made
to help people live together without hurting each
other. If we break them, we usually end up doing
something that hurts. But we have a much easier
time getting along with the rules if we think about
Jesus' rule of love. When our parents make rules
that we don't like or we read things in the Bible
that seem silly, we can ask ourselves how that
fits into the bigger rule of love. Just following
a rule doesn't always seem loving. But if we look

at the reason for the rule, then we can understand how love formed the rule in the first place.

God gave the Jewish people a lot of rules to live by. He did that because they didn't have Jesus yet, and they didn't understand a great deal about love. If you read the Old Testament carefully, you'll see that most of the time the people were more afraid of and in awe of God than anything else. That is one of the reasons Jesus came: to let people see and hear and feel God's love in person. Jesus was the Person of love. The people who lived before Jesus' time were a lot like the little toddler we were talking about awhile ago. They had to have all the rules and protections to keep them from hurting someone. After they got acquainted with Love in Person, they were wiser. They could see the reason behind all the rules. So, in a way they didn't need the rules. They wouldn't have wanted to break any of them anyhow because if they lived in love the way Jesus did, they wouldn't need rules to keep them from hurting anyone.

We still have all the rules God and our parents ever made. If we are in doubt about whether or not something will be harmful, then we can go find the rule and follow it. If you are thirteen years old and are thinking of drinking something from a bottle in the medicine chest and are not sure if it will hurt you or not, you can remember the rule: "Don't *ever* drink something from the medicine chest" that you had when you were three. Then you can put the bottle aside until you find out whether it is good for you or not.

If you aren't sure, then it is safe to follow the rule you had when you were younger. Following the rules in the Bible is the same way. If you are sure that what you are doing is loving and not harmful, then you don't need a rule. If you are not sure, then you can look up the rule and follow it.

Even if a rule seems to be very unpleasant, you can be sure that there was at one time a very good reason for it. Perhaps you have outgrown it, just as the people that Jesus talked to had. Perhaps you shouldn't need the rule at all because you are too old for it. But if you are not living love and showing it to everyone around you, perhaps your parents don't know that you have outgrown it. Maybe they think you still have to live in a playpen. Living love for everyone is the thing that shows how mature a person is. Some people need all the rules even after they are grown because they haven't learned about love yet. They haven't learned about the bigger rule that Jesus made, which isn't a rule at all but is, instead, a whole way of living. These people must follow the rules all the time to keep from getting hurt.

Nobody can live in love all the time. Nobody can follow all the rules all the time either—without some help. As we grow and learn about God, the Father, and Jesus, the Son, and about the power of the Holy Spirit, we find out that the only way to live without rules is to let God and Jesus and the Spirit live inside us and make the rule of love live inside us, too. Then the old problem of rules is solved. That doesn't happen all at once like opening the door and letting the puppy in the house. It happens gradually as we learn to give our lives over to love. Every time you act out of love, then you have grown a step toward not needing rules any longer. And every time you are not sure what is love and what isn't, then you have the good old rules to go by.

Scripture

But if you obey the voice of Yahweh your God faithfully, keeping and observing all those commandments of his that I enjoin on you today, Yahweh, your God will set you high above all the nations of the earth!—Deuteronomy 28:1

Like a bird that strays from its nest, so is the man who strays from where he belongs.—Proverbs 27:8

Even the stork in the sky knows the appropriate season; turtledove, swallow, crane, observe their time of migration.—Jeremiah 8:7

"Do not imagine that I have come to abolish the Law or the Prophets. I have come not to abolish them but to complete them. I tell you solemnly, till heaven and earth disappear, not one dot, not one little stroke, shall disappear from the Law until its purpose is achieved. . . ."—Matthew 5:17-18

Now one sabbath he happened to be taking a walk through the cornfields, and his disciples were picking ears of corn, rubbing them in their hands and eating them. Some of the Pharisees said, "Why are you doing something that is forbidden on the sabbath day?" Jesus answered them, "So you have not read what David did when he and his followers were hungry—how he went into the house of God, took the loaves of offering and ate them and gave them to his followers, loaves which only the priests are allowed to eat?" And he said to them, "The Son of Man is master of the sabbath."—Luke 6:1-6

I give you a new commandment: love one another; just as I have loved you, you also must love one another.—John 13:34

So, since the Law has no more than a reflection of these realities, and no finished picture of them, it is quite incapable of bringing the worshippers to perfection, with the same sacrifices repeatedly offered year after year. . . . He is abolishing the first sort to replace it with the second. And this will was for us to be made holy by the offering of his body made once and for all by Jesus Christ.—Hebrews 10:1 and 9-10

If I have all the eloquence of men or of angels, but speak without love, I am simply a gong booming or a cymbal clashing. If I have the gift of prophecy, understanding all the mysteries there are, and knowing everything, and if I have faith in all its fulness, to move mountains, but without love, then I am nothing at all. If I give away all that I possess, piece by piece, and if I even let them take my body to burn it, but am without love, it will do me no good whatever. . . . In short,

*there are three things that last: faith, hope, and
love; and the greatest of these is love.—1 Corinthians 13:1-3 and 13*

Chapter 14

Why Am I So Terrible?

There are two or three ways of asking that question, so when my children began asking it, I listened carefully to see what they were doing. If they were just trying to get me to disagree with them to hear me say how great they were, I wasn't interested in playing. They knew I thought they were fine young people. One of the reasons for my teaching has always been to help each individual child know that he is a unique, wonderful creation made by a purposeful, loving Creator. If I don't ever get anything else across, that is still, to me, a worthwhile accomplishment. But I don't like the game of manipulation that some people play just to get me to say some particular thing.

On the other hand, Junior High kids have a hard time with their own self-images. They aren't at all sure who they really are or how valuable. And they have watched television and read maga-

128

zines so much that they often have developed a
set of expectations that are impossibly demand-
ing. They can't help it. Their values haven't settled down and been sorted; and often there is
nobody around who will take the trouble to help
them put all the prevalent ideas into their proper
perspective. If that was what they wanted, I was
willing to go all out to help them. So I listened.

We had spent several Sundays discussing what
Jesus was like: how He approached people and
their problems; what made Him angry or sad;
what impelled Him to action. We had talked about
it enough that I was a little surprised when I realized the turn of the children's question. Was Jesus
still to them a person of long ago? I had led
them to experiences in which I was sure He had
guided us into a knowledge of His reality. Still,
this time they seemed to have lost it. When I
prayed for the Spirit to talk through me, I fully
expected Him to deal with the "Why am I so
terrible?" question from that viewpoint. But He
didn't. He approached it from an altogether different direction.

"Lord, your ways are past understanding!"

For the Junior Highs

Supposing your friend invites you to go with
him for a pizza. He says, "I know the best place
to go. They have just super good pizzas—just the
best ones I've ever eaten." He rubs his tummy
and rolls his eyes and you can hardly wait to
taste the pizza.

But then, when you get there and the waitress

serves the pizza, you are really surprised. It has the funniest things in it and the crust is different. You take a few bites and look to see how your friend is feeling. He is eating his with enthusiasm. You decide to try again. So you eat a little more. It tastes worse than the first time. How in the world, you wonder, can your friend think this pizza is the greatest in the town? You think it is terrible. The more you eat the worse it tastes until finally you give the rest of it to your friend since he seems to like it so well. You decide that the next time you'll take him where the pizza is *really* good.

You might have guessed by now that when you give your friend the kind of pizza that you like best of all in the world, he may think it is awful. Why? Well of course people's tastes differ. Not everyone likes the same thing. And I guess it's a good thing. If everyone liked the same thing best of all, we'd likely run out of it pretty soon.

And how about a flower garden? Have you ever walked through a garden with someone and listened to them "oh" and "ah" about flowers that you didn't even think were pretty, while they didn't even look at your favorites? Of course life is like that. We all know it, even when we seem to have forgotten.

Now God made each person different from each other person ever since the world began. He did that because He wanted all those different people. He didn't do it by accident, either. It would be impossible to make *everybody* different by accident. The reason He made everybody different is because He had a use for each person's characteristics. Just as your friend liked funny things in his pizza, so God seems to like funny things in His people. They are not funny to Him, though, because He knows what they are for.

When we decide that we are terrible, it is because we have a picture in our minds about what people ought to be like. Each one of us has an idea of what we'd like to be. Each one of us has a mental picture of the perfect person we think we would be perfectly happy to fit. It is a made-up picture. Part of it has come from reading books. Part has come from movies and television, and part of it has come from hearing our parents and friends say what they like. If your mother keeps telling you that she likes girls who laugh a lot and you are a very quiet, sober young lady, then you feel that you aren't a very good person. Or if your father wants you to be a scientist and you like sports or he wants you to play football and you like art, then you don't feel good about yourself. All those things and lots more go into what has made our mental pictures of what we "ought to be." If you have a clear idea of what you should be and then you find yourself not being that way, it does make you seem pretty terrible to yourself.

But let's go back to the pizza. Your friend loved all those strange things in his pizza. He even went out of his way to find a place where they served his favorite kind. He chose the very thing that you didn't like at all. It seems that he had a different picture in his mind of what good pizza

was. So he preferred what you could hardly swallow. If you were going to eat with him very much,
you would have to change your ideas and learn
to like different things.

If you are born with certain characteristics and
God is responsible because He has chosen you
to be some of the things that He wants in His
world, then maybe the problem is that you will
have to learn a different set of values. If God
wants you the way you are, He must have some
good reason. It is fun to look for the reason. It
is a good game to watch for some key to what
He had in mind when He made you the way you
are. There are some things about the way we
are that we can change it if we want to strongly
enough. And if we have learned ways of behaving
that hurt other people or ourselves, we would like
to change those. That is possible. We can ask
Jesus and the Holy Spirit to help us get rid of
bad habits. But there are some things about each
one of us that it is very hard to change. And
there are some other things that are *impossible*
to change. No matter how much I wish my fingers
were a different length, they will never be any
way but the way God made them. I had better
learn to like short fingers, if that is what I have.
Then I can see what particular job in His world
God gave my short fingers to do. Maybe it is a
very important job. Maybe my being serious or
slow-moving or overactive is very important right
now in God's creation, too, and I am missing what
I should be doing with it by worrying about it.

When Jesus said that He came that we might

have life and have it in abundance, He meant that we are to take part in whatever is good. We don't have to worry and fret and wish we were different. With Him in our lives, we can find out what we were made for and get on with doing it. God's ideas are exciting. There is no room for feeling terrible. We can choose to feel terrible—and some people do—but we don't have to. Let's all get busy right now and see if we can think of at least one reason why God might have made us just exactly as He did.

Scripture

It was you who created my inmost self, and put me together in my mother's womb; for all these mysteries I thank you; for the wonder of myself, for the wonder of your works. You know me through and through, from having watched my bones take shape when I was being formed in secret, knitted together in the limbo of the womb. . . . God, how hard it is to grasp your thoughts! How impossible to count them!—Psalm 139:13-15 and 17.

"Am I a God when near—it is Yahweh who speaks—and not one when far away? Can anyone hide in a dark corner without my seeing him? —it is Yahweh who speaks. Do I not fill heaven and earth?—it is Yahweh who speaks."—Jeremiah 23:23-24

Look at the birds in the sky. They do not sow or reap or gather into barns; yet your heavenly Father feeds them. Are you not worth much more than they are?—Matthew 6:26

Who could ever know the mind of the Lord? Who could ever be his counsellor? Who could ever give him anything or lend him anything? All that exists comes from him; all is by him and for him.—Romans 11:34-36

We are God's work of art, created in Christ Jesus to live the good life as from the beginning he had meant us to live it.—Ephesians 2:10

The word of God is something alive and active: it cuts like any double-edged sword but more finely: it can slip through the place where the soul is divided from the spirit, or joints from the marrow; it can judge the secret emotions and thoughts. No created thing can hide from him; everything is uncovered and open to the eyes of the one to whom we must give account of ourselves.—Hebrews 4:12-16

Chapter 15

What Is Eternal Life?

How can a teacher explain to children the great gift of life that Jesus gave us? Life is so undefinable, anyhow. One little seventh-grade girl said, "I think eternal life is feeling so good you never think about it." I pondered her definition for a long time. It took in the forgiveness that Jesus died to procure for us. It took in the freedom and the love and the joy that the Holy Spirit gives us. But what did she herself mean when she said "feeling so good"? I don't know. Her remark was a chance peek at something we truly do not understand.

We have so many strange mixtures of feelings about death and eternity that we hardly know what we really think. We say that because we believe in Jesus, we believe in eternal life; but our actions deny that. In our society, death is the worst enemy: dying is the ultimate tragedy.

We avoid acknowledging it and hide it. We are trapped in our denial, too. We don't deal with death as Jesus gave us permission to: as a gateway into life with Him, full of joy and light and love. Even if a child is deformed and living a life of pain, our reaction to his death is one of sadness. It is full of rage that he was cheated out of his chance at life. What if, as Jesus gave us every reason to believe, he was given his most special, beautiful gift sooner than the rest of us were? If I were to say that to most of my friends, they would raise their eyebrows and say that I was morbid. When Jesus comes into our hearts, His presence makes further life with Him the most desirable thing in the world. We love this life and don't want to part with it unseasonably. But still, the best is yet to come.

The last day of the year was supposed to be a party. We were to have brought games and puzzles. Someone had baked cookies. But we ended up crunching our goodies over the topic of eternal life. I could feel the children's unspoken puzzle. How could life, which is basically good, go on endlessly and still stay good? What had Jesus really promised us, anyhow? Did we want it? I didn't know, myself. I had not really come to terms with the basic meaning of eternal life, even though I had talked with the smaller children about heaven. I am not sure there's a difference. So when the discussion started in that direction, I found myself speaking above my own thoughts. I found myself letting the Holy Spirit speak to them and to me.

For the Junior Highs

Let's imagine that you are a little tiny child in a playpen. You have to stay in the pen in the middle of the floor while you watch your mother go from room to room and even outdoors. You can see only the room you are in. In fact, the only way that you know anything about the other rooms is by figuring out from your own tiny glimpses and from the things your mother does and says, what might be there. Since you haven't learned much nor how to understand very well, you don't get a whole lot figured out. Mostly you only guess. And because you haven't been in the rest of the house except as she has carried you, there is a great deal of exploring that you have never done.

After you have pretended all that, then imagine that you are the little child and your mother is Jesus. You are the tiny person all bounded by a fence. The fence is made up of time and space. You can't get out of time. You can't go back into the past and you can't go on into the future. You always have to stay in the right-now. And you have to stay in the place that you are in, too. You can move a little bit, but, even with airplanes, you can't be in more than one place at a time. You are limited to doing just what your body can do and only a little more which has been added by science (like hearing the music that is being played in another place over the radio or seeing pictures of activities on television that are really someplace else).

When Jesus was here, He told us that the Kingdom of God is different from this world. He didn't tell us a great deal about it, and even when He did, we didn't understand very well. It was just as if the mother of the baby in the playpen tried to explain to the baby what it would be like to go to a concert in the park. The baby couldn't understand, no matter how hard he tried. Jesus told us, though, that we would have eternal life and be with Him wherever He was going to be. Paul said, in one of his letters (which was inspired by God and not just dreamed up by Paul himself), that we'd be like Jesus when we entered into life with Him. I think he meant that we'd grow to be more and more like Him just as the little boy or girl in the playpen is growing all the time to be, eventually, a man like his father or a woman like her mother.

Jesus let us see that as soon as we take Him into our lives (which is another way of being born), then we begin to grow to be like Him. That works just like a baby who stays an individual but at the same time grows to be like his parents. As we live in love with Jesus we become more and more like him. What does that give us in our search to find out what eternal life is?

The first thing we know is that eternal life with Jesus must be centered in love. God is love and Jesus is God, so Jesus, too, is love. He doesn't just act loving. He thinks and breathes and is Himself made of love. Therefore as we grow more like Him, we grow more in love. Love, as we know, is the most powerful force in the world. Earthquakes and tornadoes and hydrogen bombs are terribly powerful. But love can come in and heal the results of their destruction. So eternal life is full of power. It is the kind of power that builds up instead of tearing down. Maybe we could say that part of eternal life is creativity, do you suppose?

Another thing we can figure out about eternal life is that it is a condition where nobody is in a playpen. We aren't fenced in by time or space. It isn't that eternal life is endless time, hour after hour. That's a way we have talked about it and even the word "eternity" has come to mean that. And, of course, lost of people, if they really thought about it, would have to admit that such a condition might be a little boring. The way Jesus' life became after He ascended into heaven was a life without any space or time at all. He can be, by the power of the Holy Spirit, everywhere at once, even back before we were born. He can be with you here and with a child in Paris at the very same instant. And He can go back into your life and heal a hurt that you had when you were three just as easily. Time just doesn't put Jesus into a playpen. Neither does space. If it did, He could only be in this room and not in the churches all over the country. Or if He were somewhere else, we couldn't have Him here with us. So, if we are to be with Jesus in the same kind of condition He is, we can assume that eternal life isn't bounded by time and space. We will be mature enough to go with Him everywhere He goes.

All of the things we have been talking about are hard to understand. If we try to draw pictures or make charts showing what eternal life is like, we will probably find that we can't even think where to begin. Still, we do have some clues right here with us. Most of us have felt love. Most of us have known what it was like to have a moment so perfect and full of love that we wished it would never end: fishing with Grandpa, maybe, or baking cookies with someone special. Maybe there has been at least once in each of our lives when things were so interesting or happy that we lost all track of time. Have you ever been so busy and caught up in what you were doing that suddenly the whole afternoon was gone? You couldn't believe it, could you?

These were just little tiny clues (like Mother gave you when you were still in your playpen and couldn't really understand what she was telling you) of what eternal life with Jesus will be. You are still so much a baby to Him that you don't always know what He means. Nobody does. Even old people get only hints of eternal life. And yet, as soon as we take Jesus into our lives, we are really living eternal life. We don't wait until we die to start. There are lots of things about what is coming that we don't know. But Jesus is just like the tiny child's mother: He helps us grow and learn and develop into adults just as fast as we can. People can be born into eternal life any time, even when they are old. But we are glad if we have had that happen when we are young so that we have a whole lot of growing time to become ready to be like Jesus. Just like the little child practicing walking around the sides of his playpen, we practice eternal life here in our present state. As we said, it has started for us when we ask Jesus into our hearts. We like practicing to be like Jesus just the way the baby likes practicing walking and talking. He doesn't know why he likes to practice. Something inside him just makes him like it.

Jesus promised us eternal life if we would turn to Him and let Him be our Friend. We know that He wouldn't promise us anything but the best. So we can be sure that whatever we *think* eternal life will be, it will be better than that. Isn't that a happy thought?

Scripture

Know then that Yahweh your God is God indeed, the faithful God who is true to his covenant and his graciousness for a thousand generations towards those who love him and keep his commandments.—Deuteronomy 7:9

The name of the city in future is to be: Yahweh-is-there.—Ezekiel 48:35

The heavens declare the glory of God, the vault of heaven proclaims his handiwork; day discourses of it to day, night to night hands on the knowledge. No utterance at all, no speech, no sound that anyone can hear; yet their voice goes out through all the earth, and their message to the ends of the world. . . The Law of Yahweh is perfect, new life for the soul; the decree of Yahweh is trustworthy, wisdom for the simple.—Psalm 19:1-5 and 7

And eternal life is this: to know you, the only true God, and Jesus Christ whom you have sent. —John 17:3

I want those you have given me to be with me where I am, so that they may always see the glory you have given me because you loved me before the foundation of the world.—John 17:24

For we know that when the tent that we live in on earth is folded up, there is a house built by God for us, an everlasting home not made by human hands, in the heavens.—2 Corinthians 5:1

He brings a new covenant, as the mediator, only so that the people who were called to an eternal inheritance may actually receive what was promised . . . —Hebrews 9:15

We know, too, that the Son of God has come, and has given us the power to know the true God. We are in the true God, as we are in his son, Jesus Christ. This is the true God, this is eternal life.—1 John 5:20

Index of Scripture